Writing to Communicate

Paragraphs and Essays

SECOND EDITION

Cynthia A. Boardman

University of California Berkeley Extension, San Francisco

Jia Frydenberg

University of California Irvine Extension
Distance Learning Center

Longman

longman.com

Writing to Communicate: Paragraphs and Essays, Second Edition

Pearson Education, 10 Bank Street, White Plains, NY 10606

Vice president, director of publishing: Allen Ascher
Editorial director: Louisa Hellegers
Acquisitions editor: Laura Le Dréan
Development editor: Andrea Bryant
Vice president, director of design and production: Rhea Banker
Director of electronic production: Aliza Greenblatt
Executive managing editor: Linda Moser
Production manager: Ray Keating
Associate production editor: Marianne Carello
Digital layout specialist: Wendy Wolf
Senior manufacturing buyer: Edith Pullman
Photo research: Mykan White
Cover design: Ann France
Cover art: Jim Starr©stockart.com
Text design: Elizabeth Carlson
Illustrators: pp. 12, 22, 24, 34, 48, 60, 82, 106, 121, 122, 152, 154, Daisy De Puthod; p. 89, Andrew
 Techiera
Photo credits: p. 1, © Bob Rowan; Progressive Image/CORBIS; p. 4, © O'Brien
 Productions/CORBIS; p. 18, AP/Wide World Photos; p. 31, Don Tremain/PhotoDisc, Inc.; p. 44,
 Izzy Schwartz/PhotoDisc, Inc.; p. 46, AP/Wide World Photos; p. 55, Geostock/PhotoDisc, Inc.;
 p. 67, © Bettmann/CORBIS; p. 77, Bob Sacha/Bob Sacha Photography; p. 80, Barbara
 Penoyar/PhotoDisc, Inc.; p. 86, © Patrick Ward/CORBIS; p. 93, AP/Wide World Photos; p. 98,
 © Reuters NewMedia Inc./CORBIS; p. 103, © Steve Chenn/CORBIS; p. 114, Bob
 Daemmrich/Stock Boston; p. 130, Corbis Digital Stock; p. 135, American Museum of Natural
 History; p. 145, Tim McCabe/USDA/NRCS/NCGC/National Cartography and Geospatial
 Center; p. 148, Laima Druskis/Pearson Education/PH College; p. 148, Barbara
 Penoyar/PhotoDisc, Inc.; p. 163, Henry Moore, "Recumbent Figure," 1938/The Tate Gallery,
 London/Art Resource, NY; p. 163, Auguste Rodin/Musee Rodin

Library of Congress Cataloging-in-Publication Data

Boardman, Cynthia A.
    Writing to communicate paragraphs and essays/Cynthia A. Boardman, Jia Frydenberg.—2nd ed.
        p. cm.
    Rev. ed. of You're in charge: writing to communicate/Gro Frydenberg, Cynthia A. Boardman.
1990.
    ISBN 0-13-027254-X (alk. paper)
    1. English language–Textbooks for foreign speakers. 2. English language–Paragraphs–
Problems, exercises, etc. 3. English language–Rhetoric–Problems, exercises, etc. 4. Academic
writing–Problems, exercises, etc. I. Frydenberg, Jia. II. Frydenberg, Jia. You're in charge.
III. Title.

PE1128 .B5938 2001
808'.042--dc21

2001029655

ISBN: 0-13-027254-X

10 11 12 13 14 15 16 BB 11 10 09 08 07

DEDICATION

For Pam, Dan, Doug and Randy

and

For Bryan

CONTENTS

TO THE TEACHER

Foundation

Welcome to the second edition of *Writing to Communicate: Paragraphs and Essays*, formerly titled *You're in Charge: Writing to Communicate*. We have been extremely pleased by the positive reaction to our book, and we have taken note of the many excellent teacher and student suggestions that have helped make this second edition an even more effective teaching tool.

There are many ways to teach writing to English-language learners. This book is based on a recursive system of writing; that is, the learners prewrite, analyze, write, revise, and rewrite. The organization of the book is also founded on the principle of scaffolding, which employs assisted progression from the known to the unknown. In addition, the book has been refocused around three main themes with several subthemes. These themes, Milestones, Ecology, and Relationships, are subjects and topics familiar to students and, as a result, discussing and writing about them will not be a large cognitive leap. The "unknown"–the type of writing to be learned within each chapter–is made more accessible to students because the subject matter is familiar.

Building on the concepts of recursiveness and scaffolding, we use a combined process and product approach to good academic writing. Each chapter sets the stage for writing with a number of introductory prewriting exercises. Second, all chapters contain specially developed models of paragraphs and essays written at the students' level of comprehension. The topics, vocabulary, and organization of the models have been carefully selected to ensure that students are able to focus on understanding *how* these are written, not struggling with *what* is written. To that end, Parts I and II contain sections about patterns of paragraph and essay writing, and Part III includes sections on graphic organizers. Also, we emphasize the process of rewriting (editing and revising). This aspect of the writing process is guided by group assignments as well as the Paragraph Checklists in Chapters 2–5 and Peer Help Worksheets in Chapters 6–14.

In the approaches mentioned above, students are active participants in the learning process. Therefore, the best use of this book is in situations where the teacher sees himself or herself more as a "facilitator" or "guide" to the learning rather than as an "oracle." Most of the exercises are open ended and can have many equally good answers. Through discussion about answers and solutions and through brainstorming and giving feedback to each others' writing, students will further develop both their ability to be critical thinkers and their writing skills. As a result, you will experience the joy of having better and better essays to read and respond to!

Audience

The book is intended to fit into the middle levels of a writing program that guides students from beginning to advanced writing of English as a Second or Foreign Language. We expect that students who use this book have had some previous experience with writing paragraph-length compositions as well as some exposure to the rhetorical structure of paragraphs. These students usually score in the 440–500 range on the paper-based TOEFL® test or 123–173 on the computer-based test. However, we have also had experience with students who score above this range who have benefited from the materials in this book.

Organization

The book is divided into three parts: Part I (Chapters 1–5) is a review of paragraph organization, Part II (Chapters 6–10) takes students step by step through the process of expanding paragraph writing to well-organized essay writing, and Part III (Chapters 11–14) introduces four rhetorical patterns of academic essay writing. There are also eight appendices, which include special writing situations, linking words, a peer help worksheet, an evaluation form, and common correction symbols.

A new feature of this second edition is that the models and exercises have been created around specific themes. This important revision has been made for two reasons: to generate excitement for the writing purpose by focusing on central issues in students' lives and to develop students' active vocabulary through the use and reuse of key words and phrases. Parts are organized around an overarching theme and the chapters within each part are organized around specific subthemes. The Contents shows the themes and subthemes for the book.

The three book parts and the chapters in those parts vary in length. When planning your course, keep in mind that the amount of time to devote to Chapters 1–10 in Parts I and II is approximately equal to the time needed for Part III by itself. Some teachers may find that they need to select exercises and assignments because they do not have time to do everything.

In addition to the textually based assignments, each chapter includes a section on the mechanics of writing.

Appendices

Many teachers want to use extra copies of three of the charts in the appendices to attach to students' work: General Peer Help Worksheet, Paragraph and Essay Evaluation, and Suggested Correction Symbols. These pages may be photocopied and distributed for classroom use.

Answer Key

An Answer Key with suggested answers to the exercises is included in the back of the book.

Questions and Comments

We welcome your comments and suggestions to this new edition of *Writing to Communicate: Paragraphs and Essays*. Please contact us through Pearson Education, 10 Bank Street, White Plains, New York, 10606

July 2001

CAB

JF

TO THE STUDENT

This book is designed to help you become a better writer of American English. It will teach you about the process of writing. This process consists of more than just picking up a pencil and writing a paragraph or an essay from beginning to end. Writing is a process because it goes through many stages. It starts with understanding what is expected of you in a writing assignment. Next, it involves thinking about what you are going to write and planning how you are going to organize it. The final steps involve writing, checking your work, and rewriting. Being a good writer means you continually change, add to, and improve what you have already written.

The major focus of this book is the organization of academic essays; that is, essays that are written in college or university classes. These essays are somewhat formal in nature and, as you will find, very direct. This style of organization may or may not be the kind that you use in your first language.

In addition to organization, you will learn other aspects of writing conventions, including punctuation, the use of linking words, and paragraph and essay format. To become a better writer, you must start with the basics of format and organization. Once these basics are under control (a process that may take a while), there is room for variation, as you will learn in later chapters.

Sometimes the hardest part of writing is deciding what you are going to say. That is why the models in this book are organized around topics familiar to most people. While you are doing the prewriting activities and reading the models, you should think about the topic and how it relates to you and your life. Then, when it's time to write, you will have some ideas about what you want to say.

Finally, most of what you learn from this book is applicable to other types of writing in English, such as business writing. By taking the time to learn the basics in this book, you will improve your overall ability to communicate in English. We hope that your experience with *Writing to Communicate: Paragraphs and Essays*, Second Edition is both a valuable and an interesting one.

ACKNOWLEDGMENTS

We would like to gratefully acknowledge our respective University of California schools: the English Language Program at Berkeley Extension in San Francisco and the Department of English and Certificate Programs for Internationals at Irvine Extension. In San Francisco, we owe a debt of gratitude to the students in the University Preparation I classes during the Fall 1999, Winter 2000, Spring 2000, and Summer 2000 sessions. Their willingness to use and comment on the drafts, as well as their sharp eyes in finding mistakes, was invaluable. We also wish to thank Jen Burton for her comments on the first draft. In Irvine, our appreciation goes particularly to Martha Compton, Linnea Hannigan, and Seija Tafoya, in addition to other instructors, for their insightful comments on various drafts.

We also wish to thank the anonymous reviewers whose feedback we incorporated into this revision. Their thoughtful suggestions contributed to our making this a better book.

Finally, we are indebted to the people at Pearson Education for their efforts in this project: Denny Lee, who was instrumental in getting the project off the ground; Louisa Hellegers, who gave us the go-ahead; and Laura Le Dréan, who held it all together through the many, many months. We also thank Andrea Bryant and Marianne Carello for their tireless efforts in making the book unified and coherent.

CAB

JF

MILESTONES

CHAPTER 1 Introduction to Academic Writing

▶ **Beginning Studies at an American University**

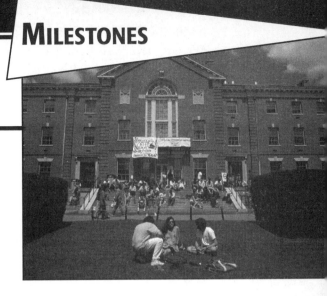

The word *milestone* is defined as "an important event or turning point in someone's life." It is a good word to describe the time in international students' lives when they have come to the United States to study English and go to an American university. As you begin this milestone, take a moment to ask yourself these questions. Then, share your thoughts with your classmates.

- Why do you want to study in the United States?

- What do you think you will like about studying here? What will you dislike?

- What do you expect from the professors? From the classes? From your classmates?

- What will *they* expect from you?

You will quickly discover that university life in the United States is probably different from what it is like in your country. What is expected from students is probably different, too. Certainly, the style of writing will be different because, after all, you will be using a different language–English. Let's begin the discussion of these differences by talking about why you write, how you write, and to whom you write in an American academic setting.

Why Do You Write?

At American colleges and universities, students are asked to write for several different purposes. Some common purposes are:

- to compare or contrast two topics

- to argue for a solution to a problem

- to describe a project

- to summarize information

- to report on a laboratory experiment or research

Students are asked to write for these purposes in a variety of academic situations, such as in composition classes and for essay tests, term papers, laboratory reports, and project reports.

How Do You Write?

In all these writing situations, students have to use a certain format and style of writing. Every student is expected to write clearly and to use correct grammar, spelling, and punctuation. Most American colleges and universities use two formats for academic writing: the **paragraph** and the **essay**. The paragraph format is used to answer test questions and to write laboratory reports. The essay format is made up of several paragraphs and is used to write compositions, term papers, and research papers.

The **style** of writing is also important. Students in the United States are expected to write in a somewhat formal style. This means that their language should be clear and direct and that they should not use slang. In addition, it is important to note that students in the United States are often expected to use their own ideas in their writing. American professors generally want their students to use original examples and arguments rather than just repeat the information they have found in their research.

Students at American universities often have very little time to do their writing. For example, some tests may require students to write several paragraphs to answer one question in a short period of time. When your time is limited, it becomes even more important not to waste any of it wondering how to say what you want to say. In addition, the organizational format used when writing in American English is often quite different from the way writing is organized in other languages. For these reasons, this book focuses on how American academic writing is organized. You will write and rewrite many paragraphs and essays. Keep in mind that the best way to improve is to practice!

To Whom Do You Write?

Since the ultimate purpose of writing is communication, all writers need to be aware of their audience, the people who will read what they write. For textbook authors, the audience is the student. For businesspeople, the audience may be a colleague or an employer (in the case of memos and reports) or a potential customer (in the case of letters and advertisements). For novelists, the audience is the general public.

The question here is: Who is the audience for students? In most cases, the audience is the teacher or professor, although, for certain reports or projects, the audience may be a classmate or classmates. However, the purpose of writing is still the same: to communicate a message. The businessperson and the student may utilize different styles and content in their writing, but they both need to be aware of their audience, and they both must work to make their message as clear as possible. Problems of clarity, organization, and even punctuation are the same for both writers.

Therefore, as you complete your writing assignments, keep in mind the classmate or teacher to whom you are writing, but remember that what you learn about academic writing will help you with any type of writing in English that you do in the future.

▶ Writing To Communicate

Read about each of these five common academic writing situations. Choose one of the assignments and write a paragraph.

1. You are a student in an art class. Your professor has asked you to describe a member of your family in detail so that the other students can draw a picture from your description. Consider the person's age, size, hair, face, and anything else that will help the other students form a picture in their mind of that person.

2. You are a student in a news writing class. Your assignment is to report on an accident, such as a car accident or a work accident, that you have seen or that you have been involved in. Since it would be difficult to write about everything that happened, make sure you include the major details. Every news story should answer the questions:

   - *Who* was involved?
   - *What* happened?
   - *Where* did it take place?
   - *When* did it happen?
   - *Why* did it occur?

3. You are taking a sociology class, and you are studying how different lifestyles influence different ways of thinking. Your assignment is to compare the way one of your parents lived when she or he was your age with the way you live now. How are your lives similar to or different from each other's?

4. You are an architecture student. Your class is studying what different people want in a house. Your assignment is to describe your dream house in as much detail as possible. Think about what your dream house shows about your personality and the way you want to live. Consider such things as its size, building materials, number of rooms, types of rooms, furniture, garden, and so on.

5. You are studying to be a science teacher for 10-year-olds. Your professor has asked you to explain one or more of the following: a simple biological process, a simple experiment, or a simple mathematical equation. Remember that a 10-year old will have to understand it. You need to be clear about the purpose and the steps involved in the subject you choose to explain.

CHAPTER 2   Types of Paragraphs

▶ Lifetime Firsts

Do you remember your first pet? Your first trip without your parents? What about your first TOEFL® test? These are all memorable because they reflect the *first* time you did something. With a group of classmates, fill in the chart with the important "firsts" in people's lives.

Childhood (birth–11 years)	
Adolescence (12–18 years)	
Young adulthood (19–25 years)	
Adulthood (26–65 years)	
Old age (older than 65)	

Your writing assignment for this chapter will focus on important firsts in your life. Circle the events in the chart that you might want to write about.

Types of Paragraphs

A **paragraph** is a group of sentences that works together to develop a main idea. Paragraphs are organized differently depending on their purpose. There are three main types of paragraphs in English: narrative, descriptive, and expository.

Narrative Paragraphs

A **narrative** paragraph tells a story. Look at this model. This is a story about one trip and what happened before, during, and after it. You can, of course, tell stories of shorter or greater length. The most important feature of a narrative paragraph is that it tells a story.

Model Paragraph 1

Europe—Here I Come

My first trip abroad was very exciting. When I was planning my trip, I looked for the cheapest airfare to Europe. Once I booked my flight, I concentrated on getting the things I needed for my month long adventure, including a passport and a Eurail pass. I decided that a backpack was the only luggage that I would need, so I bought a big one and jammed everything into it. On the day I left, I was excited and also a bit nervous because this was going to be my first trip without my parents. The flight there was much longer than I had expected, but once I arrived, I was hooked on Europe. I landed first in Amsterdam, and over the next month, I visited ten European cities from London to Rome. Everywhere I went, there were lots of young people from all over the world. We often traveled together, and we had some great times. We traveled by train and stayed in cheap hotels and youth hostels. My parents were horrified when I returned home and told them some of my stories, but I will never forget that trip. Although trips like this have become common for people of my generation, it was an unforgettable adventure for me.

What About You?

Is this story about a first trip abroad similar to your first trip without your parents either in your own country or to another country? How is it similar? How is it different?

abroad: in or to a foreign country	**a backpack**: a fairly large bag carried on your back that holds clothes and supplies	**hooked on**: addicted to, in love with
Eurail pass: a discounted ticket that allows travelers to go anywhere in Europe by train within a certain time period	**jammed**: put a lot into a small space	

This observation report is another example of a paragraph that tells a story, so it is also a narrative paragraph.

Model Paragraph 2

One Day in a Kindergarten Class

I learned a lot about planning and organizing a kindergarten class during my observation day at Matell Park Elementary School last November. At 8:00 A.M., Mrs. Anderson, the teacher, welcomed me and proudly showed me her classroom. Before the students arrived, I helped her arrange the low tables and chairs for that day's groups. At 8:15, she opened the door and let the 30 five-year-olds inside. They quietly put their bookbags away and went to sit down in a circle. Then, Mrs. Anderson greeted each child by name and asked the group what day, date, and month it was. After this, they all counted together how many days they had been in school so far. Next, she called out the names of the students and told them where to sit. At this point, her aide arrived and started helping one group with an assignment in tracing letters. Each group of five children had a different job to do. After group time, they all went to the computer room, where they practiced drawing shapes on the computer. Next was music time, and the children clapped their hands and sang a few songs. Following this, they went outside for a snack while Mrs. Anderson and I set up the room for art. When the children came back in, they were allowed to choose which art activity they wanted to do, and they went to the

What About You?

What was your first day of school like? Were you scared? Excited? Worried?

tables they had chosen. The final part of the day was story time, when Mrs. Anderson read two stories. Because of her excellent organization of both the room and the time, Mrs. Anderson taught me that 30 children can indeed learn, cooperate, behave politely, and enjoy themselves all at the same time.

an aide: a classroom helper	**to trace**: to copy something by putting paper over it and drawing what you see

Descriptive Paragraphs

The second kind of paragraph is a **descriptive** paragraph. This kind of paragraph is used to describe what something looks like. For example, you might need to describe a city for an essay about life abroad, the equipment in an experiment for a laboratory report, or a person's appearance for an essay about that person. Look at these two models. Each gives the reader a clear mental picture of what is being described. This is the goal of a descriptive paragraph.

Model Paragraph 3

My Not-So-Innocent Cat

My first little kitten has turned into a mischievous and beautiful feline. Her fur is white, which makes the perky ears on top of her head look a little pink. Her eyes are big and yellow. When she's wide awake and in trouble, they can look as bright as the sun. Her nose is pink, and under this is her mouth. It is usually open and talking or has a sly smile on it. On both sides of her mouth are whiskers. They are long and seem to dance in the sunlight. This seemingly innocent head is attached to a rather plump, but hardly lazy, body. Her legs are strong and allow her to make an escape in a matter of minutes. At the end of her body is a long tail that is constantly in motion. In short, I have to say that I love everything about this little troublemaker of mine.

What About You?

Have you ever had a pet? What kind of animal was your first pet? What did it look like?

mischievous: liking to have fun by getting into minor trouble	**a feline**: a cat or a member of the cat family	**perky**: happy and energetic **plump**: a little fat

Model Paragraph 4

Coming Home

My first trip to my ancestral hometown of Chania in Greece gave me a feeling of total peace. On the morning I arrived, the town was deserted. From my window overlooking the port, I could see a freighter off in the distance. I imagined my grandfather working as a cabin boy on a ship just like that one. On my right, the sun was streaming in through the white lace curtains fluttering in the early morning breeze. At this

What About You?

Where are your grandparents from? Have you ever been there?

time of the day, it was still a friendly sun and as bright and cheerful as my grandfather said it would be. It shone on the wooden boats pulled up on the beach below, making their pink, purple, green, and yellow colors stand out in contrast to the white sand. On my left, the harbor road curved around to the lighthouse at the tip of the peninsula. I realized that this was the same lighthouse where my great-grandfather had worked all his life. Not a car could be seen on the road, and not a single sound broke the stillness of the morning. The merchants, such as my great-aunt, had not yet opened their ocean-blue shutters, and the cafe chairs were still stacked on top of the tables with their legs pointing up to the endless sky. I had a serene feeling of being at home in a place I'd never been before.

ancestral: old, from family members from a long time ago	**a cabin boy**: a young boy who works on a ship	**shutters**: wooden coverings on the outside of a window
a port: a place where ships load and unload people and goods	**a peninsula**: a piece of land surrounded by water on three sides	**serene**: peaceful
a freighter: a ship that carries goods, not people		

Expository Paragraphs

The goal of **expository** writing is to explain something to the reader. You can explain something in many ways. Some of these are:

1. by comparing two things or people (e.g., buildings, political leaders, economic theories)

2. by showing the steps in a process (e.g., how to increase profits, how to evaluate a painting)

3. by analyzing something

   - dividing something into its parts (e.g., different theories of learning, different kinds of governments)

   - analyzing a problem (e.g., global warming, nuclear power, high divorce rates)

4. by persuading

   - trying to make others do something (e.g., stop smoking, sign a petition, join an organization)

   - arguing for your opinion (e.g., American cars vs. foreign cars, the pros and cons of giving grades in school)

Both of the following paragraphs are expository. The first explains how to do well on a standardized test. The second argues the point that teenagers shouldn't be allowed to get a driver's license until they are eighteen years old.

Model Paragraph 5

Taking the TOEFL® Test

To succeed on the TOEFL® test, which is one type of standardized test, it is important to keep certain points in mind. First, you must know the subject area well. For example, to do well on the TOEFL® test, you must be fairly fluent in English. That is, you cannot learn English just to succeed on the test. Second, you should learn the format and test-taking strategies used in the TOEFL® test. The goal of the test is to weed out nonfluent speakers, so some of the questions are tricky. If you learn the tricks, you can do better on these types of questions. Finally, it is a good idea to be rested and alert when you take the test. This means that cramming all night before the test usually doesn't help. You should arrive at the test awake and clear-headed. In sum, if you remember these three basic points, you should do well on the test.

format: the way something is organized	**to weed out**: to eliminate	**cramming**: trying to learn a lot of information very quickly
strategies: approaches used to solve problems	**tricks**: something that can fool or mislead	

Model Paragraph 6

Getting a Driver's License

In my opinion, people should be at least eighteen years old before they are allowed to get a driver's license. First of all, people under eighteen should be concentrating on their studies. It takes a lot of time for teenagers to learn the rules of the road and how to handle a vehicle. It would be better if they used this time to study. Second, statistics show that young drivers have more accidents than older drivers. They tend to be careless, and a machine that weighs several thousand pounds should be handled very seriously. Finally, and most importantly in my opinion, if teenagers cannot drive, they learn other ways to get around that may lead to good lifelong habits, such as using public transportation, bicycling, or just walking. These habits may ultimately help the environment and most certainly will help teenagers to be more physically active. In short, it is clear that there are many good reasons for a young person to wait until age eighteen to get a driver's license.

What About You?

Do you have a driver's license? How old were you when you got it?

a vehicle: a motorized machine, such as a car or a train

▶ *Practice 1* Identifying Types of Paragraphs

Identify each of these paragraphs as narrative (N), descriptive (D), or expository (E). Write the correct letter on the line after the number.

1. _____

An Old Bookcase

The old bookcase was very cluttered. On the top shelf, there were two plants. Both appeared to be dying of thirst. The second shelf had a row of old, dusty books. In front of these books were little souvenirs from various places around the world. The third shelf had a collection of trophies for many different sports: bowling, golf, tennis, and swimming. The bottom shelf was full of old magazines and newspapers. Clearly, this bookcase was a place for a lot of junk.

2. _____

A Walk on the Moon

July 21, 1969, was an unforgettable day for all the citizens of planet Earth, particularly Neil Armstrong. After traveling through space for three days, Armstrong got dressed in his space suit and prepared to take a step on the moon. The entire world was watching when he opened the door of the Apollo 11 lunar module and descended the ladder. He put his right foot on the moon's surface, and, as he did, he said the now-famous phrase, "One small step for man, one giant leap for mankind." Then, his fellow astronaut Buzz Aldrin joined him. Together, they performed scientific experiments and also had some fun entertaining the world with their lunar antics. Since that day, several other men have walked on the moon, but none inspired a whole world in quite the same way.

3. _____

An Island of History

Ellis Island is part of an interesting chapter in U.S. history. The federal government bought it in 1808. At first, it was used as a fort. Later on, the army used it to store weapons. Then, in 1891, it became the place that it is now famous for being. The government made it a gateway for immigrants to the United States. More than 12 million immigrants passed through Ellis Island between 1892 and 1954. It closed in November of 1954. At the end of the twentieth century, it reopened as a tourist attraction. Today, both American and foreign tourists go there to learn about the big role that this small island played in U.S. history.

4. _____

Football vs. Rugby

American football and rugby have more differences than similarities. For instance, football requires eleven players, whereas rugby requires thirteen to fifteen. Also, a football field is longer than a rugby field but is less wide. Football has four quarters of fifteen minutes each, but rugby has two forty-minute halves. A touchdown in football is worth six points; however, a goal in rugby is worth four points. There are also a few basic similarities. Both games are played with a leather, oval-shaped ball, and both are based on soccer. In short, while football and rugby have some similarities, their differences help make them two unique games.

5. _____

A Child's Face

The child's face reflected her cheerful and determined nature. Her hair was bright red and had a royal-blue bow tied at the top. The skin on her forehead, as well as her entire face, was soft white and covered with freckles. Her eyes were a sparkling blue and, at that moment, were focused on the end of her turned-up nose. Her lips were a pretty pink, and coming from between them was a tongue stretching to its limit in an upward direction. It was clear that she was determined to touch her tongue to her nose, perhaps simply to prove to herself that it could be done.

Mechanics

Paragraph Format

When you write a paragraph in English, you must use correct paragraph format. Follow the example below.

	Name
	Date
	Title
	The first sentence of your paragraph must be indented
	five spaces. Do not start each sentence on a new line.
	Each sentence begins where the sentence before it ended.
	The rest of the lines should start at the left margin.
	Margins on both sides of the page should be about an inch.
	Begin each sentence with a capital letter, and end each
	sentence with correct punctuation — a period, a question
	mark, or an exclamation point. Also, you should double-
	space your paragraph. This means writing on every other
	line. Finally, center your title on the first line, and add your
	name and the date in the upper right-hand corner.

There are five points to note about this paragraph.

1. The first sentence begins five spaces to the right. This is called indentation. Most paragraphs are indented. That way, we know where one paragraph ends and another begins. Longer pieces of writing, such as essays, have several paragraphs and therefore several paragraph indentations.

2. Next, sentences always start with a capital letter and end with a period, a question mark, or an exclamation point.

3. The third point is that each sentence begins where the previous sentence ends. A new sentence does not automatically begin on the next line.

4. Another important point is to write on every other line. This is called double-spacing. It may not always be necessary to double-space on tests, but it is usually necessary on compositions and term papers.

5. Finally, remember that there should be margins around a paragraph. There should be about one inch of space on each side of the paper.

Some teachers still accept handwritten papers, but many prefer that you do your work on a computer. There are additional considerations for writing on the computer, which you can find in Appendix 3 on page 172.

The Writing Process—Part 1

Good writers think, plan, write a draft, think, rewrite, think, and rewrite until they are satisfied. Writing is a continuous process of thinking and organizing, rethinking and reorganizing. Good writers go through six basic steps. Each step can be repeated as many times as necessary. This chapter discusses the first four steps. Chapter 3 describes the last two steps.

Step 1: Assessing the Assignment

Every college or university class is going to have writing assignments with different purposes, so the first step in the writing process is to understand exactly what the professor wants on a particular assignment. The most important piece of information for you to know is the topic (or range of topics) and purpose of the assignment.

Another important point is to know the sources of information that you may use. In other words, where should the information in your writing assignment come from? In advanced writing classes and many content-based classes, you will be expected to do research. For other classes, you will use your own background knowledge. This can include your feelings and opinions about topics. (For the writing assignments in this book, you shouldn't do research. The source of information should be your own ideas, knowledge, and thoughts.) Finally, you need to be clear on the length of the paper, its due date, and its format.

Let's say that you are taking an early childhood education class. It's the first day of class and your professor wants you to write "a short paragraph describing your first day at school." What do you need to know? Here are some questions students might ask and answers the professor might give.

- What is the purpose of this assignment?—*To think about and explore your own experience of school at an early age so that you will remember how it feels for young children on their first day of school.*

- Should I do research?—*No, this is about your memory of your experience.*
- How short is short?—*One page; ten to fifteen sentences.*
- When must I turn in this paragraph?—*Next class.*
- Can I write it by hand, or does it need to be typed?—*Typed.*

Step 2: Generating Ideas

The purpose of this step is to think about a certain topic and generate as many ideas as possible. (Even when you get information from other sources, you still need to take this step to figure out what kind of information you need to look for.) There are many ways to do this; two of the most effective are brainstorming and freewriting.

Brainstorming

Brainstorming can be done individually or in groups. The purpose of **brainstorming** is to think about and write down a lot of ideas without worrying about what they are, how they are ordered, or even whether you will use them. If a small group is formed, one person may be made the recorder of the group. As all the members of the group come up with ideas about what they can write for the assignment, the recorder takes notes to share with the group later. Each student can also take his or her own notes. It is important to note all the ideas. This is not the time to evaluate how good or bad they are.

Look at this example of notes from a brainstorming session about a person's first day at school.

first day – preschool - 4 years old – don't remember

kindergarten – 5 yrs - ?

first grade – 6 yrs old – teacher Mrs. Grant

Dad took me – Mom was sick

scared, didn't want to leave sick mom

New school, new kids – one boy pulled my hair

holding Dad's hand tightly – didn't want to let go

trying not to cry

Mrs. Grant was nice, though

Dad left me there, promised to come back – he was late

my own desk – lots of crayons

kids all around – coloring made lots of noise

chocolate kiss in lunch bag from Mom – felt better

Freewriting

Freewriting is similar to brainstorming. You start with a word or a phrase and write down anything you can think of that is related to the topic. Unlike brainstorming, you don't just list a lot of points; instead, you try to write sentences in which one word leads to the next. When you get stuck, you just pick up on one of the previous words and continue writing about that. You don't have to worry about grammar, punctuation, or spelling because no one will see your freewriting but you. The most important aspect of freewriting is *not to allow yourself to stop*. If you practice freewriting, you will find that some words tend to be repeated and that ideas occur to you just from writing those words. Just let your ideas and imagination flow.

Here is an example of freewriting. It is also about a person's first day of school.

> I really can't remember my very first day of school. I
> remember Mrs. Grant though in first grade she was nice
> ~~~~ but I was ~~~~ scared because my mom was sick
> She couldn't take me to school ~~~~ I had to go with my
> dad. One boy was very mean. he kept pulling my hair. I
> remember that Mrs. Grant made us all be quiet ~~~~ we
> were coloring. It was a loud noise!!!!!!!!! I found a chocolate
> kiss in my lunch bag. Mom was sick but she was thinking of
> me. I wanted ~~~~ to go home because I was tired ~~~~
> my dad was late. I cried for the first time all day.

Step 3: Organizing Your Ideas

Step 2 shows how to get some ideas for your paragraph. Now, you need to organize those ideas. Two methods to help you organize are topic outlines and tree diagrams.

Topic Outline

One way to organize your ideas is to outline the points you want to make. To write a **topic outline**, you first have to decide what the main idea of the paragraph is. You should write that idea as a sentence or just as a few words on the top of your paper. After that, you need to consider which points to include in order to best support your main point. You should pick the best ones from your brainstorming or freewriting and list them on separate lines below your main point. In an outline, you don't have to use complete sentences. All you need are a few words that will help you remember what you are going to write. Like brainstorming and freewriting, an outline is just for you, not for anybody else. Look at the example of a topic outline below that is based on the previous brainstorming and freewriting.

My first day of school was good and bad.
    I. The good stuff
        A. Mrs. Grant
        B. Coloring
            1. lots of crayons
            2. impressive noise of all the kids
               working
        C. chocolate kiss in lunch
    II. The bad stuff
        A. Mom sick
        B. Boy pulled my hair
        C. Dad late
        D. I cried

Tree Diagram

Some people prefer a more visual kind of outline format called a **tree diagram**. You start with the main idea and then make branches to points that support your idea. Look at this example of a tree diagram that also organizes the information about the first day of school.

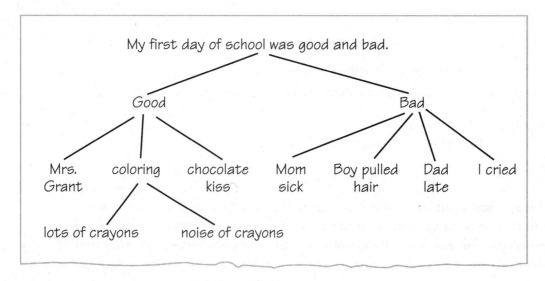

Step 4: Writing the First Draft

Once you have your ideas generated and an organizational pattern to follow, you can write your first draft. Here is an example of a first draft of the paragraph about the first day of school.

> My first day of school was both good and bad. One of the good things was my teacher Mrs. Grant. She was very nice. Another good part of that day was when Mrs. Grant had us all be quiet and listen to the sound of the crayons while we were coloring. I was surprised that it was such a loud noise. The last good memory that I have of that day is finding the chocolate kiss in my lunch bag. It made me remember that my mom loved me. There were bad things, too. The worst was that my mom was sick and couldn't take me to school. I didn't want to leave her alone, but my dad insisted that we go to school. One boy there kept pulling my hair. Then, my dad was late picking me up, and I cried. I'm glad I don't have to relive that day.

This is a first draft because it is not finished yet. Good writers should make sure to read their writing carefully in order to make changes and corrections before they consider it finished. The process of making these changes will be discussed in Chapter 3.

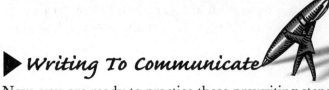

▶ Writing To Communicate

Now, you are ready to practice these prewriting steps. Go back to page 4 and look at the list of lifetime firsts that you circled. Choose one and prepare to write a paragraph about it.

In order to complete the process described in "Step 1: Assessing the Assignment" on page 11, you need to know that your writing assignment should be about one page long, it should contain only your ideas, and you should use correct paragraph format.

▶ Practice 2   Generating Ideas

Generate your ideas in this space by brainstorming or freewriting for ten minutes.

_____

_____

_____

_____

▶ Practice 3   Organizing

Now organize your paragraph. Use either the topic outline or the tree diagram format.

• **Topic Outline**

Main idea

_____

_____

Supporting points

_____

_____

_____

_____

• Tree Diagram

▶ *Practice 4*   **Writing a First Draft**

Now, you are ready to write your first draft. Remember to use correct paragraph format.

Paragraph Checklist

It is always a good idea to set your paragraph aside for a while after you have written it, and then go back and reread it. Use this Paragraph Checklist as a guide for what to look for when you reread your paragraph. Check off the items that are true for your paragraph.

Paragraph Checklist

1 ▶ I have indented my paragraph. . . . . ❏

2 ▶ Each of my sentences begins with a capital letter and ends with a period, a question mark, or an exclamation point. . . . . ❏

3 ▶ Each of my sentences begins where the previous sentence ended. . . . . . ❏

4 ▶ I have double-spaced my paragraph. . . . . ❏

5 ▶ I have appropriate margins on both sides of my page. . . . . ❏

If any of the items are not checked off, correct your paragraph, and then complete the checklist.

CHAPTER 3 Organization of Paragraphs

Holidays

Many holidays observed around the world are important for two reasons. First, holidays are special days that bring family and friends together. Second, holidays usually commemorate, or remind us of, a significant time in history. For these reasons, holidays can be milestones in people's lives.

How can we classify commemorative holidays? There are national holidays, religious holidays, and other types of holidays. With a classmate, fill in the chart with examples of each type of holiday. Then, circle your favorite holiday.

	The United States	Other Countries
National holidays		
Religious holidays		
Others		

Basic Organization

Paragraphs have a very specific organizational pattern. By this, we mean that all paragraphs are put together in a similar way and use the same three basic parts: topic sentence, body, and concluding sentence. When you follow this pattern, your paragraph will be easy for your reader to understand. Look at this model paragraph.

Model Paragraph 1

Ways to Celebrate New Year's Eve

topic
sentence

[body]

People in the United States celebrate New Year's Eve in many ways. [The most common way may be going to a big party with lots of friends, music, and dancing. At the stroke of midnight, people at these parties grab their sweethearts and spend the first seconds of the new year kissing them. Another way to spend New Year's Eve is with the significant other in your life. The new year is greeted with a champagne toast to the relationship. Sometimes, families with children like to spend the evening together, letting the "kids" stay up until midnight. Finally, some people like to spend the evening by themselves. They use this time to evaluate the past year and to make resolutions and plans for the coming year. It is a time of reflection that can only happen when one is alone.] In short, New Year's Eve is a special time that can be spent with friends, with family, or even alone.

concluding
sentence

to grab: to take hold of quickly and strongly	**a significant other**: a spouse, girlfriend, or boyfriend	**a resolution**: a promise that you make to yourself

This paragraph begins with a sentence that introduces the topic and main idea of the paragraph. It is called the topic sentence. The middle part of the paragraph is called the body, and it consists of sentences that explain, or support, the topic sentence. These sentences are called supporting sentences. The last sentence is called the concluding sentence, which ends the paragraph by reminding the reader of the main point of the paragraph.

Paragraphs can stand alone or they can be parts of longer pieces of writing, such as essays. When they stand alone, they almost always consist of these three parts, but when they are part of a longer piece of writing, there can be many variations in their style. These variations will be discussed in Chapter 10. However, basic academic writing in the United States is linear in structure; that is, it has a beginning, a middle, and an end, and it continues directly from one part to the next. Once you have mastered this organizational pattern, you will be able to use it in all types of writing in English.

The Topic Sentence

A **topic sentence** is the most important sentence in a paragraph because it contains the main idea of the paragraph. A good topic sentence has two parts: the topic and the controlling idea. The **topic** is the subject of your paragraph. It is what you are writing about. The **controlling idea** limits the topic of your paragraph to the aspect of that topic that you want to explore in your paragraph. Look at these examples:

1. New York is a fun place to be on New Year's Eve.
   topic   *controlling idea*

2. New York has great entertainment.
   topic   *controlling idea*

3. New York is the world's most famous city.
   topic   *controlling idea*

Each of these topic sentences has the same topic, New York, but a different controlling idea. Each one would introduce a distinct paragraph with different ideas and information. The possibilities for writing about New York are practically endless, so this one topic could have many controlling ideas. Therefore, you could write many different paragraphs about New York.

It is important to keep in mind that most academic writing is done to persuade the reader that a point of view is reasonable. Therefore, another important part of writing topic sentences is to write a sentence that has a clear point of view. This usually means that the topic sentence contains the opinion or attitude of the writer. A statement of fact is not an effective topic sentence because there is nothing more that can be said about it and, therefore, nothing to write in your paragraph. Look at these two sentences:

4. Twenty-five people attended the company's Halloween party.

5. The company's Halloween party was a bore, as usual.

Sentence (4) is not an effective topic sentence because it is a fact. It is difficult to write more about facts because they are either true or false. However, since sentence (5) is an opinion, there is a lot the writer could say to convince the reader that the party was a bore. Therefore, it is an acceptable topic sentence.

Another common way to write a topic sentence is to divide a topic into different parts. Look at these three sentences:

6. <u>Ramadan</u> has (three important days within the month of fasting.)
   topic   *controlling idea*

7. There are three main kinds of holidays.

8. Planning a good Fourth of July party requires five specific steps.

For each of these topic sentences, the writer explains the division of the topic into parts. That explanation is the controlling idea. Circle the controlling ideas in numbers 7 and 8.

▶ *Practice 1* Identifying Topics and Controlling Ideas

Read each sentence. Underline the topic and circle the controlling idea.

1. Alcohol is harmful to your health.

2. The Western world should have a holiday to recognize senior citizens.

3. The colors of the U.S. flag have unique symbolic meanings.

4. A camping vacation sounds like a punishment to me.

5. Weeds can ruin a vegetable garden.

▶ *Practice 2* Evaluating Topic Sentences

Read each sentence and decide if it is a good topic sentence. Remember that topic sentences should state an opinion or divide the topic into parts. If the sentence is a good topic sentence, underline the topic and circle the controlling idea. If it isn't, cross it out.

1. American education has five stages.

2. My brother is older than I am.

3. Writing a good résumé takes a lot of hard work.

4. Jack is Kate's friend.

5. Jack is Kate's best friend.

6. You need four ingredients to make peanut butter.

7. Big business is threatening the environment.

8. Big business has an effect on the environment.

9. Cats are also called felines.

10. There are many reasons to visit San Francisco.

► *Practice 3* **Writing Topic Sentences**

This chart contains general topics and possible controlling ideas. Choose a controlling idea, and write a topic sentence. One example for each topic has been done for you.

Topics	Possible Controlling Ideas	Example Topic Sentence	Your Topic Sentence
Christmas	• overcommercialized • depressing • time for family and friends • exciting	Seeing Christmas decorations in October is a sign that Christmas has become over-commercialized.	_____ _____ _____ _____ _____ _____
First day at school	• joyful • uneventful • difficult	My first day at kindergarten was much more difficult than my first day at college.	_____ _____ _____ _____ _____ _____
First car	• unreliable • beautiful • freedom	Despite what everyone said, my first car was the most beautiful car I had ever seen.	_____ _____ _____ _____ _____ _____

The Body (Supporting Sentences)

In terms of content, the **supporting sentences** support the topic sentence. One of the most common ways to support a topic sentence is to use **facts** or **statistics**.

Model Paragraph 2 ──────────────

An Expensive Holiday

Valentine's Day is a very expensive holiday. Typically, people who are in love with each other exchange gifts. The gifts often cost a lot of money, sometimes as much as $100. In some cases, if you don't spend that much, your sweetheart might think you don't care. Some less expensive gifts that people often give are chocolate and flowers. One pound of good chocolate may cost $10 to $15, and when you add up all of the chocolate that is sold on Valentine's Day, the total is probably well over $1 million. Flowers cost more than chocolate, so sales of flowers may amount to $5 million! Also, it is often expected that you and your sweetheart will go out to dinner on that evening. A romantic dinner at a nice restaurant may cost $100 or more per person. It seems to me that Valentine's Day is one of the most expensive days of the year.

A second way to support a topic sentence is with **examples**.

Model Paragraph 3

Valentine's Day Overload

Usually three or four weeks before Valentine's Day, you begin to see too many reminders of this only-for-lovers holiday almost everywhere. For example, you see red hearts and cupids in every shop and restaurant. Shops want you to buy a gift for your Valentine, and restaurants hope that you will treat yourself and your Valentine to an expensive dinner. You also seem to see more pictures of people in love and more people on the streets who are obviously in love. They walk hand-in-hand and gaze into each other's eyes lovingly. Another example of Valentine's Day reminders is seeing the commercials on TV, which tell you about all the wonderful presents and cards that you can buy for that "special someone." In short, we are constantly reminded of Valentine's Day for several weeks each year.

overload: too many things at the same time	**a cupid**: a representation of the Roman god of love, usually shown as a small winged boy with a bow and arrow	**hand-in-hand**: holding hands **to gaze**: to look at something or someone for a long time

The third common way of supporting a topic sentence is by using an illustration that is based on a **personal experience**. This paragraph relates a personal experience about Valentine's Day.

Model Paragraph 4

A Sad Valentine

Valentine's Day makes people feel bad if they are alone. Last Valentine's Day, I was alone because I had broken up with my boyfriend the week before. On that Valentine's night, I was expecting roses and chocolates from him when he took me out to a romantic dinner, but instead I stayed in and ate a frozen pizza and a candy bar in front of the TV while I looked at my artificial flowers. I was so upset. Then, I found the present that I was going to give him on Valentine's Day. It was a cute teddy bear holding a big heart that said, "I love you!" As I held it, I realized that the only Valentine card I had received was from my grandmother. I started to cry and wondered how many other people felt as bad as I did. It's clear that Valentine's Day can only be a happy day if you have someone special to share it with.

artificial: not natural	**a teddy bear**: a soft toy shaped like a bear

Major and Minor Supporting Sentences

In terms of organization, especially of expository paragraphs, there are two types of supporting sentences: major supporting sentences and minor supporting sentences. The **major supporting sentences** are the main details that tell us about the topic sentence. The **minor supporting sentences** tell us more about the major supporting sentences.

Look again at the paragraph "Ways to Celebrate New Year's Eve" on page 18. Below, it has been diagrammed to show the parts of a paragraph, including the major and minor supporting sentences.

Topic Sentence (TS)

▶ People in the United States celebrate New Year's Eve in many ways.

Major Supporting Sentence (SS)

▶ The most common way may be going to a big party with lots of friends, music, and dancing.

Minor Supporting Sentence (ss)

▶ At the stroke of midnight, people at these parties grab their sweethearts and spend the first seconds of the new year kissing them.

Major Supporting Sentence (SS)

▶ Another way to spend New Year's Eve is with the significant other in your life.

Minor Supporting Sentence (ss)

▶ The new year is greeted with a champagne toast to the relationship.

Major Supporting Sentence (SS)

▶ Sometimes, families with children like to spend the evening together, letting the kids stay up until midnight.

Major Supporting Sentence (SS)

▶ Finally, some people like to spend the evening by themselves.

Minor Supporting Sentence (ss)

▶ They use this time to evaluate the past year and to make resolutions and plans for the coming year.

Minor Supporting Sentence (ss)

▶ It is a time of reflection that can only happen when one is alone.

Concluding Sentence (CS)

▶ In short, New Year's Eve is a special time that can be spent with friends, with family, or even alone.

It is important to note that all major supporting sentences do *not* need to have the same number of minor supporting sentences. In fact, sometimes you will not have any minor supporting sentences at all.

▶ *Practice 4*   Diagramming a Paragraph

Diagram the paragraph "Valentine's Day Overload" on page 22. Indicate the major supporting sentences and the minor supporting sentences. Use the example on this page as a guide.

The Concluding Sentence

The **concluding sentence** of a paragraph is generally a **restatement** of the topic sentence. It may not be possible to restate the topic itself, but it is always possible to restate the controlling idea. Look at this paragraph and pay particular attention to the topic sentence and its restatement in the concluding sentence.

Model Paragraph 5 ————————————————————————

How to Carve a Pumpkin

With Halloween just around the corner, it's good to know how to carve a pumpkin. The first step is to gather your materials. You'll need a large pumpkin, a sharp carving knife, a big spoon, a black marking pen, a candle, and some newspaper. Spread the newspaper on a table and place the pumpkin on top of it. Using the knife, cut off the top of the pumpkin. Then, use the spoon to take out the seeds from

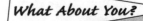

What About You?

Is there a holiday like Halloween in your country? Is there a time of year to celebrate the harvest?

the inside the pumpkin. Next, with the marking pen, draw eyes, a nose, and a mouth on one side of the pumpkin in shapes that can be cut out. The next step is to carefully cut out the eyes, nose, and mouth with the knife. Put a lighted candle inside the pumpkin, and put the top back on the pumpkin. Finally, put it in a window after dark on Halloween night. Once you know how to carve a pumpkin, you can amuse your trick-or-treaters this year and every year.

around the corner: happening soon	**a trick-or-treater**: a child dressed in a costume who goes from house to house on Halloween asking for candy
to gather: to collect	

A second, less common, way to conclude a paragraph is to write a sentence that **summarizes** the main points in the body of the paragraph.

Model Paragraph 6 ————————————————————————

Celebrating the New Year

The new year is celebrated throughout the world at many different times, based on the solar or lunar calendar. January 1 is recognized throughout the world as the beginning of the new year, but this date is the beginning of the Christian year based on the Gregorian solar calendar. The Jewish new year is called Rosh Hashanah and is celebrated in September or October even though the Hebrew calendar is lunar. The Chinese new year, called Tet in Vietnam, follows a lunar calendar and comes on a day between January 10 and February 19 according to the solar calendar. Islam also uses a lunar calendar. Its new year celebration is in the spring, and the date varies depending on the year. In short, Christians use the solar calendar, whereas Jews, Chinese, Vietnamese, and Muslims use a lunar calendar to determine when to celebrate the new year.

solar: related to the sun	**lunar**: related to the moon

Read these topic sentences from Practice 3 on page 21. Write restatement concluding sentences for each.

1. Seeing Christmas decorations in October is a sign that Christmas has become overcommercialized.

   _____

2. My first day at kindergarten was much more difficult than my first day at college.

   _____

3. Despite what everyone said, my first car was the most beautiful car I had ever seen.

   _____

Mechanics

Punctuation Marks

The use of punctuation marks varies greatly from language to language. In academic writing in English, the rules of punctuation must be followed carefully.

To use punctuation marks correctly, you must have a basic understanding of sentence structure. A sentence must have an **independent clause**. Look at the meanings of these words to help you understand what an independent clause is.

independent: able to stand alone; not dependent on something else

clause: a group of words containing a subject and a verb

independent clause: a group of words that contains a subject and a verb and that can stand alone

Note that the basic punctuation pattern for a sentence is to begin it with a capital letter and end it with a period.

Examples

Sentence (there is an independent clause)

> St. Patrick's Day honors Irish-Americans.
> *subject   verb*

Not a sentence (there is no independent clause)

> When Irish-Americans are honored on St. Patrick's Day
> *This is not independent because we don't know what happens when Irish-Americans are honored.*

> Honoring Irish-Americans on St. Patrick's Day
> *This is not independent because <u>honoring</u> is not a verb with a tense. It's a gerund or participle.*

► *Practice 6* Identifying Sentences

Read each group of words and decide whether it is a sentence. If it is, put a capital letter at the beginning and a period at the end. If it isn't, cross it out.

1. in the United States religious holidays often become nonreligious

2. the government of the United States recognizes eight holidays by giving its employees the day off

3. the parents hiding several hundred Easter eggs

4. when we spent a long holiday weekend in the mountains

5. most people look forward to long holiday weekends

Using Commas: Coordinating Conjunctions

You can combine two independent clauses into one by using a comma and a **coordinating conjunction**. Coordinating conjunctions are words that establish a relationship between two independent clauses. There are seven coordinating conjunctions, and you can easily remember them by remembering the word *FANBOYS*.

F=for A=and N=nor B=but O=or Y=yet S=so

When these words are used to connect independent clauses, they are preceded by a comma.

Examples

There are four major food groups, *and* it is important to eat something from each one every day.

They know a lot about nutrition, *yet* they eat unhealthy food.

It was pouring rain, *so* we decided to go to a movie.

We can't go out, *nor* can we stay home. [*Note:* When we use *nor* in this way, we must use question word order after it.]

There are two further points to note about this punctuation pattern:

- It is important to remember that the part of the sentence that comes after the coordinating conjunction is an independent clause with a subject and a verb. If it doesn't have a subject and verb, do not use a comma.
  ### Example
  Annie got up late *and* forgot to call her mother on Mother's Day.

- Although you may see coordinating conjunctions begin a sentence after a period, it is not considered good academic style to use them in that position. Using a transition with the same meaning is preferable. (Chapter 4 discusses transitions.)

Examples
Nonacademic style

We were going to go to the movie. But, we didn't know what time it started.

Academic style

We were going to go to the movie. However, we didn't know what time it started.

▶ *Practice 7* **Combining Sentences with Coordinating Conjunctions**

Combine the pairs of sentences with an appropriate coordinating conjunction. Be sure to use a comma between the sentences. Try to use each coordinating conjunction only once. More than one correct answer is possible.

1. David is allergic to cats. He doesn't have one.

   _____

2. You can have cereal for breakfast. You can have eggs for breakfast.

   _____

3. Ken loves to celebrate New Year's Eve. He's too sick to go out this year.

   _____

4. The roses in the garden are dying. They aren't getting enough water.

   _____

5. The sun isn't shining brightly. It isn't completely hidden.

   _____

6. Katy went to Colorado. She rafted down the Colorado River.

   _____

7. The bird is looking for small branches to build a nest. She can't find any.

   _____

The Writing Process—Part 2

In Chapter 2, you learned about the first four steps in the writing process.

   Step 1: Assessing the Assignment

   Step 2: Generating Ideas

   Step 3: Organizing Your Ideas

   Step 4: Writing the First Draft

Now, you will learn about Steps 5 and 6.

Step 5: Rewriting

Rewriting is a critical part of the writing process and consists of two separate processes: revising and editing.

Revising

Revising is the first part of rewriting. You may start revising as soon as you finish writing, or, better yet, set your paragraph aside for a while and go back to it later. Read what you have written, and ask yourself these questions: "Have I said what I wanted to say?" and "Have I made myself clear to the reader?" These are questions about the content of your writing. As you revise, you also need to ask yourself about the organization of your paragraph. The basic questions to ask are: "Does this paragraph have a topic sentence?", "What is my topic?", "What is my controlling idea?", "What are my major supports?", "Do I need more minor supports?", and "Do I have a concluding sentence?"

▶ *Practice 8* Evaluating Revised Paragraphs

Here is the first draft of the paragraph from Chapter 2 on page 15. Read the paragraph and the writer's notes. Then, read the revised paragraph that follows. Note the changes that the writer has made. Are there any other changes you would make either to the content or the organization? Discuss these with your classmates.

First Draft Paragraph

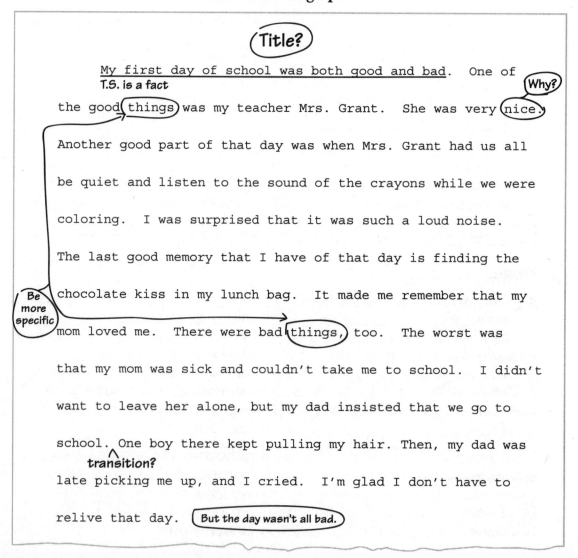

Revised Paragraph

A Good Start

My first day of school was more good than bad. One of the good memories of that day was my teacher Mrs. Grant. She was very nice and seemed to understand why all the children were a little scared. Another good part of that day was when Mrs. Grant had us all be quiet and listen to the sound of the crayons while we were coloring. I was surprised that it was such a loud noise. The last good memory that I have of that day is finding the chocolate kiss in my lunch bag. It made me remember that my mom loved me. I also have a few memories of being frightened. My mom was sick and couldn't take me to school. I didn't want to leave her alone, but my dad insisted that we go to school. Also, my dad was late picking me up, and I cried. However, looking back, I was glad to be in my new adventure at school.

The content of the revised paragraph has greatly improved. Note that the topic sentence now has an opinion that is supported. The overall organization is much tighter, too, because the body of the paragraph has clear major supporting sentences and minor supporting sentences. Even the concluding sentence is stronger. In addition, this paragraph now has a suitable title.

Editing

The other aspect of rewriting is **editing**. When you edit, you check to make sure the spelling, capitalization, punctuation, vocabulary, and grammar are correct. Editing is somewhat mechanical because you are basically following rules. The rules of spelling, for example, are clear; a word is either right or wrong. In grammar and punctuation as well, we can usually say that something is wrong and something else is right. Your classmates and your teacher can help you write better and more correctly by using editing symbols to give you feedback. You can find a list of some of these symbols in Appendix 8, page 181.

There may also be times when you or your teacher will feel that one sentence is better than another, even though there is nothing grammatically wrong with the original sentence. This is the area where revising and editing meet. Becoming a better writer is a process of combining these two aspects of rewriting in order to best communicate what you want the reader to understand.

Step 6: Writing the Final Draft

Writing the final draft is the last step in the writing process. Keep in mind that any of the steps can be repeated at any time. This is especially true for Steps 3, 4, and 5. Don't forget to write your final draft using correct paragraph format. Be sure to add a title.

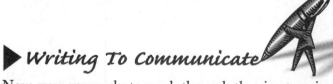

▶ *Writing To Communicate*

Now, you are ready to work through the six steps in the writing process to write a paragraph. Choose one of the holidays you circled on page 18 or one of the topic sentences you wrote for Practice 3 on page 21. Generate ideas by brainstorming or freewriting. Next, do a simple outline or tree diagram. Then, write the first draft of your paragraph. Put it aside for at least an hour, and then continue with the writing process by revising and editing your paragraph. Finally, write the final draft of your paragraph using correct paragraph format.

Paragraph Checklist

Use this Paragraph Checklist as a guide to review the organization of your paragraph. Check off the items that are true. If any of the items are *not* checked off, correct your paragraph, then complete the checklist.

Paragraph Checklist
1 ▶ I have a topic sentence that contains the main idea of my paragraph. . . . . ❑
2 ▶ I have underlined the topic and circled the controlling idea. . . . . ❑

3 ▶ The body of my paragraph consists of:
(Check one.)
    Facts or statistics. . . . . ❑
    Examples. . . . . ❑
    An illustration based on personal experience. . . . . ❑

4 ▶ I have major supporting sentences. Some of them are supported by minor supporting sentences. . . . . ❑

5 ▶ My concluding sentence:
(Check one.)
    Restates the topic sentence. . . . . ❑
    Summarizes the main points of the body of the paragraph. . . . . ❑

CHAPTER 4 Coherence and Cohesion

▶

Passages of Life

Regardless of culture, all people experience "passages of life." The details of these passages will vary greatly depending on a person's culture and background. For example, the first passage of life is birth. In the United States, even before a baby is born, its birth is celebrated with a baby shower. A baby shower is a party where people give gifts for the baby to the mother-to-be. After the baby is born, people may give more presents and the parents often hold a religious ceremony called a baptism or a christening. How does your culture welcome new babies?

With a partner, fill in the timeline with the common passages of life that people experience. Then, share with your partner any rituals or customs in your culture that are commonly associated with each passage of life.

●——●

birth   *death*

Coherence

So far, you have learned about the different types of paragraphs and their organization. All good paragraphs also have some characteristics in common. The first of these is called **coherence**. A coherent paragraph is made up of sentences that are ordered according to a principle. The principle changes depending on the type of paragraph that you are writing. The three types of ordering are chronological ordering, spatial ordering, and logical ordering.

Narrative Paragraphs and Chronological Ordering

For a narrative paragraph, you must use good **chronological ordering** of sentences. This means that the supporting sentences must tell the events of a story in the order that they happened. In other words, the events must be ordered according to time. The following paragraph tells about an important event in any child's life. It clearly tells the story of one day as it happened through time–from waking up in the early morning to finding the birthday present at the end of the day.

The Best Birthday

My eleventh birthday was the best of my childhood. I awoke early in the morning and found my room was decorated in my favorite colors—black and orange for my favorite sports team. After I got dressed, I went downstairs. I had to pass the dining room on my way to the kitchen, so I saw all my birthday presents piled high on the table. I rushed into the kitchen, and my mother greeted me with a big kiss. I begged her to let me open just one present, but she said I had to wait until later, when all my aunts and uncles would arrive. The day seemed endless while I waited. At last, my aunts and uncles arrived in the late afternoon. Then, my mother said I could open my presents. I tore into each colorfully wrapped present, but I was disappointed because each package contained only a piece of paper with one word written on it. My mother knew I liked puzzles, so she said that this was a puzzle I had to figure out. I looked at all the words and realized that my real present was in the garage. When I ran out there, I saw my beautiful new ten-speed bicycle. I was thrilled and told them all that I would never forget this wonderful day.

What About You?

Do you remember one birthday better than the rest? How old were you? Why was it so special?

piled high: things put on top of one another	**wrapped**: having paper or cloth around something to cover it	**a puzzle**: a game or problem that requires thinking to figure out

Descriptive Paragraphs and Spatial Ordering

Descriptive paragraphs also need good coherence, or good ordering of sentences. However, they do not use chronological ordering. They use **spatial ordering**. In other words, they have sentences that are ordered according to space. Usually, this means that items are described systematically through space. For example, this could be top to bottom, head to foot, left to right, or front to back.

The following paragraph describes a person on a special day. We usually think about how a person looks from head to toe, so a good writer will use spatial ordering from top to bottom to describe a person. The idea is to help the reader understand the paragraph by mentally picturing what is being described.

Model Paragraph 2

A Beautiful Bride

Sue looked picture-perfect on her wedding day. Her short, dark hair had been curled for the occasion, and on top of it rested a small veil. Under her naturally arched eyebrows, her warm brown eyes reflected serenity. Her eyes had only the slightest bit of makeup on them, as usual. Her straight nose seemed to indicate that she was headed in the right direction. Her cheeks were rosy, and her lips were naturally red and full. She stood straight as an arrow as she walked down the aisle on the arm of her father. She wore a short, white, elegant dress and held a bouquet of white gardenias. Her stride was confident, yet formal, and made in white sandals. Indeed, Sue looked beautiful as she walked toward her new husband and her new life.

a veil: a thin piece of material a bride often wears that covers her face **arched**: curved	**serenity**: peacefulness **an aisle**: a long passage between the rows of seats in a church (or theater or plane, etc.)	**a gardenia**: a type of white flower with a strong fragrance **a stride**: a long step you take when you walk

Expository Paragraphs and Logical Ordering

As you might guess by now, expository paragraphs also require good coherence. The principle, however, is different. With expository paragraphs, coherence is based on logic or reason. We call this **logical ordering** of sentences in a paragraph. Look at the following model of an expository paragraph. The ordering of the supporting sentences follows a logical pattern in that each celebration is described before another is mentioned. Also, the religious celebrations are discussed before the nonreligious ones, and the two are not mixed.

Model Paragraph 3

Becoming an Adult

There are many ways that societies welcome children into adulthood. For example, in many Native American tribes, adolescents are sent on a vision quest. This is a time when they go off on their own to find a personal spirit to guide them through life. Another example of children passing on to adulthood is celebrated in Judaism. When boys and girls turn thirteen, they are allowed to read the Torah in the synagogue and are then accepted as adults. In Catholicism, boys and girls have their confirmation ceremony. In this ceremony, they pledge themselves, as adults, to the church and to Christ. There are non-religious rites of passage, too. "Sweet Sixteen" parties are very popular, as are *quinceañeras* parties for Latina girls. Even getting a driver's license can mean that a child has become an adult in many countries. In short, then, the common thread in all these activities is the recognition that a child is old enough to be treated as an adult and to assume adult responsibilities.

a tribe: a group of people of the same race who have the same beliefs and customs and who live in the same area **Torah**: the holy book of Jewish people	**a synagogue**: a building where Jewish people worship **Latina**: term used to refer to girls or women whose cultural background is based in a Spanish-speaking country, such as Mexico	**quinceañeras**: literally, fifteen years; a party for fifteen year old girls in Latino cultures **a common thread**: a similar feature

▶ *Practice 1* Working with Coherence

Identify each of these paragraphs as narrative (N), descriptive (D), or expository (E). Write the correct letter on the line after the number. Then, circle the sentence that is out of order and draw an arrow to indicate where it should go. The first one has been done as an example.

1. ___E___

A Ten-Speed vs. a Tricycle

Ten-speed bicycles and tricycles are both people-powered means of transportation, but there are obvious differences. The first difference is in the number of wheels. Of course, this difference in the number of wheels is due to the difference in the kind of rider. A ten-speed bicycle has two wheels, whereas a tricycle has three wheels. A ten-speed is ridden by someone who is able to balance a bicycle on two wheels. On the other hand, a tricycle is ridden by someone who doesn't have this skill. The final obvious difference between a ten-speed and a tricycle is that a ten-speed has ten gears. It is designed to do many kinds of riding, but a tricycle has only one speed and offers one kind of riding. In conclusion, ten-speeds and tricycles have differences that are easy to see at a glance.

2. _____

A Birthday Piñata

The piñata at my niece's birthday party was the familiar donkey-shaped one. The head had two bright red ears that stood straight up. The red nose was long and under it was the neck of the "donkey." The body was plump and hid the tummy full of candy. It was striped in red and green. The ears had green earrings. The legs looked like stumps on a tree but were pink in color. The tail was really just red, green, and pink ribbon that had been cut long and curled. The parts of the piñata that my niece no doubt remembers best, however, are the many brightly colored pieces of candy that fell from it after she hit it squarely in the middle and broke it. It was a typical piñata destroyed in a typical way.

3. _____

An Anniversary to Remember

Few couples reach their seventy-fifth wedding anniversary, but my grandparents did last year, and they celebrated in an unusual, but quite romantic, way. First, they renewed their wedding vows in the same place and at the same time that they had been married all those years earlier. This meant that we all had to be at City Hall at 6:30 in the morning. That evening, we went dancing at the old Starlight Room downtown. Then, as they had done, we went to breakfast at the Maple Leaf Restaurant. Perhaps this was a great place for breakfast seventy-five years ago, but, in my opinion, it wasn't anymore. Still, my grandparents looked happy eating the meal of fried eggs and bacon that they had eaten all those years ago. In the afternoon, we went to a matinee at the Roxie Theater. The owners of the theater had even managed to find out what was playing the day of their wedding, so we watched the same movie they had. At the end of the evening, my grandparents spent their second "wedding night" in the same room of the same hotel where they had spent their first. All in all, it was one of the most romantic days of my life, and it wasn't even my anniversary!

What About You?

Do older people that you know still celebrate their anniversary in a romantic way? What do they do?

4. _____

The Instruments of an Orchestra

The modern orchestra is divided into four distinct groups. The first group is the strings. Their sound is produced by vibrating strings or wires. Woodwind instruments make up the second section of an orchestra. These instruments, such as flutes, piccolos, and oboes, make their sound by the player blowing into a mouthpiece and opening and closing holes in the instrument. The third section is the brass section, whose instruments make sounds by the vibration of the player's lips on a mouthpiece. Examples of brass instruments are bugles, trumpets, and tubas. Examples of string instruments are violins, cellos, and basses. The last section of an orchestra is the percussion section. The sound of these instruments is made by hitting them. Examples of percussion instruments include cymbals, drums, and tambourines. When put together, these four groups of instruments make a complete orchestra.

Cohesion

Another characteristic of a good paragraph is **cohesion**. When a paragraph has cohesion, all the supporting sentences "stick together" in their support of the topic sentence. The methods of connecting sentences to each other are called **cohesive devices**. Five important cohesive devices are linking words, personal pronouns, definite articles, demonstrative pronouns, and synonyms.

Linking Words

There are many ways to help give a paragraph cohesion. One way is to use **linking words**. There are many kinds of linking words: coordinating conjunctions (which were discussed in Chapter 3), subordinating conjunctions, prepositions, and transitions. **Transitions** are a very common type of linking word. They are words or phrases that help to connect sentences to one another. They may also help the coherence of a paragraph by indicating the order of the supporting sentences. To some extent, linking words, including transitions, are particular to the type of paragraph that you are writing. The chart below lists some common linking words for each type of paragraph. Appendix 5 on pages 177–178 provides a more complete listing of common linking words.

Paragraph Type	Transitions	Other Linking Words
Narrative	first, second, third, etc. at first next after that later on then finally	in the morning in the afternoon in the evening until then
Descriptive		to the left to the right in front of behind on top of under above next to
Expository	first, second, third, etc. however on the other hand in fact for example therefore furthermore finally in short in conclusion	

Look at the paragraphs on pages 32–33 and underline the words and phrases that connect the sentences in the paragraphs.

Personal Pronouns

Another way to help a paragraph have good cohesion is by using **personal pronouns**. Pronouns usually have antecedents, or nouns that they stand for, in previous sentence parts or sentences. In other words, a pronoun usually refers back to a previous noun–its antecedent. For example:

The little boy looked at the birthday cake.

He stuck out *his* finger and took a taste of *it*.

Using the personal pronouns *he*, *his*, and *it* in the second sentence connects these two sentences. In fact, if you didn't use pronouns, you would have an awkward second sentence that might not seem related to the first one. For example:

The little boy looked at the birthday cake.

The little boy stuck out the little boy's finger and took a taste of the birthday cake.

The Definite Article

A third way to connect sentences is to use the **definite article** *the*. A noun with a definite article often relates to a previously mentioned noun. For example:

I bought an anniversary present yesterday.

The anniversary present is for my grandparents.

It's obvious that these two sentences are talking about the same anniversary present because of the use of the definite article in the second sentence. In fact, if the definite article were not used, these two sentences would not be related. Look at these two sentences:

I bought an anniversary present yesterday.

An anniversary present is for my grandparents.

Demonstrative Pronouns

Another way to connect sentences in a paragraph, or to give a paragraph good cohesion, is to use the **demonstrative pronouns** *this*, *that*, *these*, and *those*. Like previous cohesive devices, demonstrative pronouns require antecedents in order to help connect sentences to those that came before. For example:

On top of the table was a present.

This present had purple wrapping paper.

You could also use the definite article instead of the demonstrative pronoun to indicate that the two sentences go together. However, you must use one or the other. If you don't, then these two sentences aren't connected. For example:

On top of the table was a present.

A present had purple wrapping paper.

Synonyms

The use of **synonyms** is also a cohesive device in that the synonyms refer back to their antecedents. Like using a pronoun, using a synonym also prevents the frequent repetition of a word or words. Read the first paragraph. It is awkward because of the overrepetition of words. Then read the revised version using synonyms for the forms of *depress* and *retire*.

Retirement

The sixty-five-year-old employee was *depressed* at the thought of his <u>retirement</u>. His boss told him that he had to <u>retire</u> because he was at <u>retirement</u> age, but he didn't want to <u>retire</u>. Therefore, he became *depressed*. He thought that his days would be *depressing* from then on because he was <u>retired</u>. In fact, he was so *depressed* that his wife made him find another job with a company that didn't have a <u>retirement</u> age. He wasn't *depressed* after that.

Retirement (Revised Version)

The employee was *saddened* by the thought of his retirement. His boss told him that he had to <u>stop working</u> because he was sixty-five, but he felt that he still had a lot of good work years in him. He didn't want to <u>quit working</u>, so he became depressed. He thought that his days would become *boring and useless* from then on because he <u>couldn't work</u>. In fact, he became so *distressed* that his wife made him find a company to work for that didn't have a retirement policy. He felt great after that.

In the revised paragraph, the cohesive devices are useful in relating sentences in a paragraph to one another. When sentences are related, a paragraph has good cohesion.

▶ *Practice 2*   **Working with Cohesive Devices**

This paragraph lacks cohesion because it doesn't have linking words, definite articles, or demonstrative pronouns. It also repeats nouns instead of using personal pronouns or synonyms. Rewrite the paragraph on a separate piece of paper. Make the cohesion better.

Preparing to Travel

Traveling to a foreign city can be fun, but traveling to a foreign city requires some planning besides getting a passport. You should buy a phrase book and learn a few key phrases in a foreign language. Using phrases demonstrates a willingness to learn about the people who live in a foreign city. Read about a city beforehand. Read about what places in a foreign city you'd like to see. Get a feeling for a foreign city and for weather so that you can pack appropriate clothes. Check your camera. Make sure that your camera is in good working order and that you have lots of film. Get yourself a good pair of walking shoes, and break a good pair of walking shoes in for about a month before you leave. Taking a few precautions before you leave can make your trip to a foreign city more enjoyable.

Mechanics

Using Commas: Transitions and Adverbial Clauses

When a word, a phrase, or a dependent clause comes before an independent clause, we use a comma after it and before the independent clause. Words and phrases that are used in this way are called transitions, and dependent clauses that are common in this pattern are called adverbial clauses.

Transitions

As you have read earlier in this chapter, **transitions** are linking words because they make connections between sentences. The use of the comma is different with transitions than it is with coordinating conjunctions (see Chapter 3). Many transitions can go at the beginning, in the middle, or at the end of a sentence, but no matter where they are, they are *set off* from the rest of the sentence by commas.

Examples

For example, Memorial Day honors soldiers who died in wars.

OR

Memorial Day, for example, honors soldiers who died in wars.

OR

Memorial Day honors soldiers who died in wars, for example.

There are many transition words and phrases in English. Here are some of the most common ones and their meanings. A more complete list is provided in Appendix 5 on pages 177–178.

Example	Chronology	Result	Difference	Addition	Conclusion
for example for instance	after that later on first, second, etc. next then	consequently as a result therefore	however in contrast on the other hand	moreover in addition furthermore	in conclusion in short all in all

There are two further points to note about this punctuation pattern:

- If the transition is a short, single-syllable transition, and it comes at the beginning of a sentence, it is acceptable to eliminate the comma.

Examples

First, we went to the movies.

OR

First we went to the movies.

- The use of *for example* and *such as* can be confusing. *For example* is a transition, so a complete sentence (with a subject and a verb) must follow it. Use *such as*, preceded by a comma, if you want to make a list of words and phrases. See the examples on page 40.

Examples

There are many memorials for soldiers in the United States. *For example*, the USS *Arizona* honors soldiers who died at Pearl Harbor at the beginning of World War II.

OR

There are many memorials for soldiers in the United States, *such as* the USS *Arizona*, the Korean Veterans Memorial and the Vietnam Veterans Memorial.

▶ *Practice 3* **Combining Sentences Using Transitions**

Connect the pairs of sentences by using one of the transitions in the chart on page 39. Vary the position of the transition.

1. The Pacific Ocean has many forms of life. There are fish, plants, and microscopic organisms.

    _____

2. I dragged myself out of bed. I took a cold shower to wake myself up.

    _____

3. December is a winter month in the Northern Hemisphere. December is a summer month in the Southern Hemisphere.

    _____

4. The volcano erupted for ten days. The village at the bottom of it was destroyed.

    _____

5. If you want to enjoy a long holiday weekend, you need to leave for your destination early. You need to come back home early.

    _____

Adverbial Clauses

An **adverbial clause** is a type of dependent clause. It has a special relationship with an independent clause. This relationship is determined by a **subordinator**, or **subordinating conjunction**, the word or phrase that connects the two clauses. When a sentence begins with an adverbial clause, there must be a comma between this clause and the main, or independent, clause. For example:

*   Because he was sixty-five, he was forced to retire.
*   If I have enough time, I will make a cake for the retirement party.
*   Although he loved his job, the company forced him to retire.

However, when the adverbial clause comes after the independent clause, we do not use a comma. Look at the rewritten sentences in which the adverbial clause comes after the independent clause.

- He was forced to retire <u>because he was sixty-five</u>.
- I will make a cake for the retirement party <u>if I have enough time</u>.
- The company forced him to retire <u>although he loved his job</u>.

As with transitions, there are many subordinators. Here are some of the most common ones.

Chronology	Causation	Unexpected Result	Difference	Condition
after before while when until	because since	although even though	whereas while	if

There is one exception to the comma rule above. When an adverbial clause beginning with the subordinators *while* and *whereas* comes after an independent clause, use a comma.

Examples

Labor Day is celebrated in September in the United States, *while* it is celebrated in May in most other countries in the world.

Some businesses recognize Martin Luther King Jr. Day as a holiday, *whereas* other businesses do not.

▶ *Practice 4*   Combining Clauses

Combine the pairs of sentences by making one an adverbial clause. Vary the position of the adverbial clause and use a comma when necessary.

1. Monday is the Fourth of July. We don't have to go to work.

   _____

2. Fireworks are standard for holiday celebrations. I don't like them.

   _____

3. It is foggy and cold near the ocean. It is sunny and hot inland.

   _____

4. Betty baked some Christmas cookies. She took them to her neighbor.

   _____

5. There will soon be too many people in the world. People keep having babies.

   _____

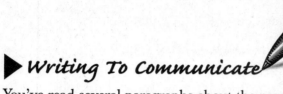

▶ Writing To Communicate

You've read several paragraphs about the passages of life in this chapter, and now it's your turn to write one. Look at the suggested topics that follow. Choose one that brings back a pleasant memory, and freewrite for about ten minutes. Remember that freewriting is a way of generating ideas. Write down everything that comes into your mind, and don't worry about spelling or grammar. If one topic seems too difficult, move on to another. Just get your ideas on paper. Here are some suggested topics:

- your favorite childhood birthday, a wedding you attended, an anniversary or retirement party you attended (narrative)

- clothing worn in a passage-of-life ceremony in your culture or the place where one occurs (descriptive)

- different ways of welcoming a baby to the world or different types of weddings (expository)

Now organize your ideas into a paragraph with a clear topic sentence, supporting sentences, and a concluding sentence. Be sure to order your supporting sentences so that your paragraph has good coherence and to use linking words, pronouns, definite articles, demonstrative pronouns, and synonyms where appropriate so your paragraph has good cohesion.

After you have written your paragraph in the correct paragraph format for your teacher, rewrite it so that each of the sentences is on a separate line. After you are finished, cut your paragraph sentences into strips so that each strip has one sentence on it. Mix your sentences up and exchange them with a classmate's. Put each other's sentences in the correct order. If you or your classmate has trouble arranging the sentences, discuss what should be changed in the sentences to make them easier to put in order.

Paragraph Checklist

Use this Paragraph Checklist as a guide to check your paragraph for good coherence and correct use of cohesive devises. Check off the items that are true. If any of the items are *not* checked off, correct your paragraph, then complete the checklist. If you need an explanation of any of the terms, review the chapter.

Paragraph Checklist

1. ▶ I have a topic sentence. .... ☐

2. ▶ I have underlined the topic and circled the controlling idea. .... ☐

3. ▶ My paragraph has good coherence. It follows:
   (Check one.)
   Chronological order .... ☐
   Spatial order .... ☐
   Logical order .... ☐

4. ▶ My paragraph has good cohesion between sentences.
   I have used the following cohesive devices:
   (Check all that apply.)
   Linking words .... ☐
   Personal pronouns .... ☐
   Definite article .... ☐
   Demonstrative pronouns .... ☐
   Synonyms .... ☐

CHAPTER 5 Unity and Completeness

▶

Events in U.S. History

The history of any country is full of milestones: the election of a new leader, the death of a member of the royal family, a war of independence, even a scientific invention or discovery. With a partner or on your own, identify five of the most important milestones in your country's history.

1. _____

2. _____

3. _____

4. _____

5. _____

Share your list with your classmates. Are any of your events the same as or parallel with your classmates' events?

Your writing assignment for this chapter will focus on an event or a person in your country's history. Circle the two events on your list that you might want to write about.

Unity

As you have seen, a good paragraph must have three separate parts: a topic sentence, supporting sentences, and a concluding sentence. It must also have certain characteristics, such as coherence and cohesion. Another paragraph characteristic is **unity**. When a paragraph has unity, all the supporting sentences relate to the topic sentence. Look at the following paragraph. Read each of the supporting sentences carefully.

A National Treasure

The Smithsonian Institute, located in Washington, D.C., was established in 1846 for two reasons. The first was to do fundamental research and then publish the findings of this research. This research is used by historians and scientists all over the world. The second reason was to preserve the history and culture of the United States. The Smithsonian Institute established a museum to do this. The original building still stands today and is called the Smithsonian Museum. Since that first museum, many more have been built to house artifacts from various areas of U.S. society and history. Some of the most famous of these museums are the

National Air and Space Museum, the National Gallery of Art, and the National Museum of Natural History. <u>The president of the United States also lives in Washington, D.C.</u> These two functions of the Smithsonian Institute continue to be very important to the American people.

fundamental: basic	**to preserve**: to keep something from being harmed, destroyed, or changed	**an artifact**: something studied by scientists that was made and used a long time ago.

Since this is a paragraph about the Smithsonian Institute, all the sentences should talk about that. However, the underlined sentence about the president of the United States is not about the Smithsonian Institute. Therefore, it does not belong in this paragraph and should be crossed out. A sentence that does not belong in a paragraph is called an **irrelevant sentence**.

▶ *Practice 1*   **Finding Irrelevant Sentences**

Find the irrelevant sentences and cross them out so that the paragraph will be unified.

1.   **Two Similar Canals**

    The Suez Canal and the Panama Canal have similar histories. Today, many tourists visit both canals. The same Frenchman, Ferdinand de Lesseps, controlled the initial building of both canals. The Suez Canal was begun in 1859 by the Suez Canal Company. This company, which completed the project in 1869, was controlled by the French. Likewise, the French bought a Colombian canal-building company in 1881 in order to build the Panama Canal. Americans finally finished that canal. In the end, however, both canals finally came under control of the countries in which they are located. Egypt gained control of the Suez Canal in 1957 by fighting France and Britain. Panama gained control over its canal peaceably in 1977. These similar events took place about twenty years apart and provided the world with two important waterways.

2.   **A Woman of Strength**

    The strength of character that Eleanor Roosevelt possessed was obvious in her face. On her head, which was always held high, her light hair was styled in a no-nonsense way and did not cover her forehead or eyes. Her eyebrows were thick and natural, and

What About You?

Who are some famous women in your country's history? Why are they famous?

under these were her intense eyes, which revealed her intelligent mind. Her nose
was straight, and, as she aged, her cheeks sagged a bit and
formed the common wrinkles that make a triangle out of the
nose and edges of the mouth. She was a serious woman, but,
when she smiled, her smile showed sincerity and genuine
pleasure. She was a great asset to her husband, Franklin, who
was president of the United States from 1932 to 1945. In
short, it was clear from the first impression that Eleanor
Roosevelt was a strong woman.

▶ *Practice 2* Evaluating Paragraphs for Unity

**This exercise is similar to the previous one, but it is a little bit more difficult. Continue
to look for irrelevant sentences, but note that there may be more than one in each
paragraph or there may not be any. Cross out all the irrelevant sentences that you find.**

1.   **Difficult Years**

My father grew up during a difficult time in U.S. history called the
Depression. It occurred after the crash of the stock market in 1929, when my
father was ten years old. Many people lost their businesses and their money, and
my father's family was no different. The restaurant they owned closed because no
one could afford to eat out. They had very little money, and my father often had
little or nothing to eat during the day. Some millionaires killed themselves because
they lost all their money. He had one pair of shoes, which he had gotten from his
father. He wore the shoes for many years and put cardboard or newspaper in the
soles when they got holes in them. During this time of economic hardship, like
many people, my father and his parents lost their home, too. They had to live in a
two-room apartment with his aunt and uncle and their three kids. All in all, the
Depression years were hard years for most people, including my father.

2.   **The First Disneyland**

The original Disneyland changed the idea of what a family amusement park
should be. First of all, it was really several mini-parks in one. There was
Fantasyland, which was full of children's favorite cartoon characters. There is also

a Fantasyland at Disney World in Florida. Frontierland attracted the older children and some adults with its wild west theme. Tomorrowland gave adults a look into the future with its many exhibits of products of the future. Next, there were many different kinds of rides. Young children could go with Peter Pan on a ride to Never-Never Land, or they could ride the horses on the carousel. Every teenager loved to "drive" the cars on the freeways of the future, and for teenagers and adults alike there was the roller-coaster ride called the Matterhorn. Now, of course, there are many more roller coasters in Disneyland, such as Space Mountain and Thunder Mountain. Finally, there were all the stores on Main Street. Nowhere else could you buy Disney cartoon characters or Disney souvenirs of all kinds and prices. In short, the amusement parks of today owe it all to the original Disneyland.

3.   **A Beacon of Freedom**

The Statue of Liberty must have been a welcoming sight for the many immigrants who came to the United States at the end of the nineteenth century. She stands in the middle of New York Harbor and is over 300 feet tall. Her right hand is raised as far as it can be and is holding a torch that is made of gold, so it looks like a light at the end of a long journey. On top of her head is a crown with several spikes around the edge of the crown. It almost looks like a halo, and, indeed, she was considered an angel to many foreigners seeking a new life. The look on her face is strong and loving and, to some, may have the look of a mother welcoming her children home. In her left hand, she holds a book, and at her feet are broken chains, which symbolize the freedom that so many immigrants came to this country looking for. Even the message carved on the pedestal holding the statue is one that calls people from all over the world to come to this land. The Statue of Liberty certainly must have made a lasting impression on all the people who came to the United States looking for a better life.

Completeness

Another characteristic of a good paragraph is **completeness**. Your paragraph is complete when it has all the major supporting sentences it needs to fully explain the topic sentence and all the minor supporting sentences it needs to explain each major supporting sentence. A paragraph that is not complete does not have enough sentences to follow through on what the topic sentence promises.

Look at the paragraph and pay particular attention to the topic sentence. Why do you think this paragraph is not complete?

Edison and His Inventions

Thomas Alva Edison is famous for his many useful inventions. The most useful certainly has to be the electric lightbulb. Before this invention, people had to light their homes after dark with candles or gas lighting. Both of these could be dangerous. Another one of Edison's inventions was the motion picture projector. This invention was the beginning of the movie business, which employs millions of people and entertains millions more. In short, Edison contributed a lot to the world through his inventions.

The topic sentence says that Thomas Edison created *many* inventions, but only two are discussed. The word *many* means at least three, so in order for this paragraph to be complete, we would need to talk about at least one more invention.

Sometimes, whether or not a paragraph is complete isn't quite so obvious. Look at the following paragraph. It is not complete either, but the reason isn't as apparent as in the previous paragraph.

The Kite and the Thunderstorm

Nearly every American child has heard the story of Ben Franklin and his famous kite experiment. Franklin wanted to prove that lightning was really electricity. One night, there was a bad thunderstorm. Since there was also a lot of lightning, Franklin thought that this was the right time to prove his theory. He put a key on the string of a kite and went outside to fly the kite in the storm. The jolt of electricity from the lightning knocked Franklin off his feet. At that point, he knew his theory was right. People probably began telling the story the next day, and they have been telling it ever since.

This paragraph is somewhat confusing because an important part of the story is missing. The writer needs to add the step in the experiment where the lightning bolt hits the key. If that step is added, the paragraph will be complete.

▶ *Practice 3* **Evaluating Paragraphs for Completeness**

Read each of the following paragraphs. Decide whether or not it is complete. When a paragraph isn't complete, add a sentence or sentences that would make it complete.

1.   **A Country at War**

Of all the international conflicts that the United States was involved in during the twentieth century, only two were officially declared as wars. The first declared war was, of course, World War I, which happened early in the century. After

Congress passed an act of war, the United States became part of the Associated Powers, which fought against the Central Powers, which included Germany and Austria-Hungary. Other international conflicts referred to as wars (the Korean War and the Vietnam War) were never official wars. In addition, during the 1980s and 1990s, the United States sent its armed forces to many areas of the world, including Africa, the Middle East, Asia, and Eastern Europe, but these actions were mostly in support of UN efforts to establish peace in these regions. In short, it seems the United States became involved in a lot of military action in the twentieth century—sometimes officially and sometimes not.

2.   **The Sights of San Francisco**

If you are planning to visit San Francisco, there are several places that you shouldn't miss. Probably the most famous sight is the Golden Gate Bridge. It was built in 1937 and is still as striking today as it was then. Golden Gate Park is also a lovely place to visit on a nice day. The De Young Museum as well as the Japanese Tea Garden are located there. You must visit Fisherman's Wharf, where you can eat a delicious meal of your favorite seafood. Chinatown on Grant Street is famous for its good food, too. In addition, if you want great chocolate, Ghiradelli Square is the place to go. These attractions and many more have made San Francisco the popular tourist place that it is.

3.   **The Pony Express**

In 1860, Pony Express riders were loved because they delivered mail in the United States relatively quickly, but their job was very difficult. A typical day for a rider began before sunrise. He took the mail pouch and rode at a horse's full speed for twenty-five miles to the next station. Then, he jumped off the tired horse and jumped on another one. There was no time for him to stop and talk or even eat. He had to ride another twenty-five miles to the next station. By the end of the day, he had covered seventy-five miles. Only then could he rest and eat and get ready for the next day. It was grueling work, and the job ceased to exist in late 1861.

Mechanics

Fragments

As you learned in Chapter 3, the minimum sentence in written English consists of a subject and a verb and is an independent clause. (The only exception to this rule is an imperative sentence. In the case of an imperative, the sentence has a "hidden subject.") Strings of words that either do not have a subject or do not have a verb are called **fragments** and must be corrected. Another kind of fragment is a dependent clause that is not connected to an independent clause. Look at these fragments:

1. Because I needed to buy milk.

2. John singing in the shower.

3. Dancing and laughing on our way home from the party.

4. For example, a computer.

Fragments should never be used in academic writing. Here are some ways to correct the preceding fragments.

1. "Because I needed to buy milk" is a dependent clause. A dependent clause must be connected to an independent clause. You, the writer, must decide whether it should be connected to the sentence in front of it or the sentence after it. Possible corrections are:

   Because I needed to buy milk, I went to the store.

   OR

   I went to the store because I needed to buy milk.

2. In "John singing in the shower," *singing* is a form of a verb, but it does not have a tense. There are three forms of a verb in English that do not have a tense: the present participle, the past participle, and the infinitive. *Singing* is the present participle of the verb *sing*. To make this fragment into a sentence, you need to change the present participle to a verb with a tense. Possible corrections are:

   John was singing in the shower.

   OR

   John sings in the shower.

3. "Dancing and laughing on our way home from the party" is a fragment because it does not have a subject. In addition, the verbs are present participles. Possible corrections are:

   We were dancing and laughing on our way home from the party.

   OR

   We danced and laughed on our way home from the party.

   OR

   Dancing and laughing on our way home from the party, we woke up all the neighbors.

4. "For example, a computer" has only a noun phrase (*a computer*) and no verb. You need to add a verb and to decide if the noun phrase is the subject or object of the sentence. Possible corrections are:

For example, a computer is useful for writing papers.

OR

For example, I think having a computer is useful.

▶ *Practice 4* Identifying Fragments

This paragraph has five fragments. Find them and correct them.

The History of Baseball

Modern baseball has an interesting history. Actually started out in England as a game called *rounders*. It made its way to North America and was largely played in rural areas. By 1830, most urban and rural area teams that played together, but there were still no official rules or even a standard playing area. When a group in New York City published a book in 1845. It gave baseball twenty rules, two teams of nine players each and defined the playing field. Simply called the New York game. Its popularity continued to grow, and during the Civil War in the 1860s, the Yankee soldiers spread the game throughout the country. By the end of the 1860s. The name had changed to baseball and it looked very much like the game we know today.

Reviewing Coherence, Cohesion, Unity, and Completeness

You have learned a lot of new words and concepts in Chapters 4 and 5 of this book. Take a few minutes to review them by doing this practice.

▶ *Practice 5* Analyzing a Paragraph

Evaluate the paragraph on page 52 by answering the questions and making the necessary corrections.

1. Does the paragraph have coherence? Move any sentences that are out of order.

2. Does the paragraph have cohesion? Underline the cohesive devices.

3. Does the paragraph have unity? Cross out any irrelevant sentences.

4. Does the paragraph have completeness? Add any necessary sentences.

Revolutions of the Sixties

The 1960s was a time of many social revolutions in the United States. The first one was the civil rights movement. This was begun in earnest in the early sixties by the black people in the country, who were tired of being treated as second-class citizens. They demanded to be treated equally to the white majority in the country. Martin Luther King and Malcolm X were two vocal leaders of this movement. Both men were killed by assassins. Another social revolution was happening for the women in the country. This movement was called women's liberation. Women, too, were demanding equality with men in the workplace and at home. They wanted to be paid the same salaries and have the same job opportunities as men, and they wanted to share the household tasks and the raising of children with the men in their lives. The final social revolution in the sixties was the sexual revolution. Birth control methods were becoming more available and more acceptable, and people realized that they could have sex without the fear of pregnancy. Young people were also fighting against their parents' generation and its idea that people had to be married before having sex. In conclusion, many social movements that affect U.S. society in important ways began in the 1960s.

▶ Writing To Communicate

At the beginning of Part I, you imagined that you were in a university class and that you had to write a short paragraph. Now, imagine that you are in a world history class and that your professor wants you to write about an aspect of your country's history. Choose one of these assignments.

- Explain your country's participation in a war.
- Write about the life of an important person and/or inventor in your country's history.
- Describe an important building or monument in your country.
- Explain about an important day, year, or decade in your country's history.

Follow the writing process: assess the assignment, generate ideas, organize your ideas, write your first draft, rewrite, and write your final draft in correct paragraph format.

Paragraph Checklist

Use this Paragraph Checklist as you go through the rewriting step of the writing process. If any of the items are *not* checked off, correct your paragraph, then complete the checklist.

Paragraph Checklist

1 I have a topic sentence at the beginning of my paragraph.
I underlined the topic and circled the controlling idea. . . . . ☐

2 My paragraph follows:
(Check one.)

  Chronological ordering . . . . ☐
  Spatial ordering . . . . ☐
  Logical ordering . . . . ☐

3 My paragraph has unity. There are no irrelevant sentences. . . . . ☐

4 My paragraph is complete. There are no missing parts. . . . . ☐

5 I have used correct paragraph format, including
indentation and margins. . . . . ☐

CHAPTER 6   From Paragraph to Essay

ECOLOGY

Animals in Their Ecosystems

The word *ecology* is defined as "the relationship between organisms (such as plants, animals, and people) and their environment." All animals prefer to live in certain environments. A polar bear would rather live in the North Pole than in San Diego, and a rattlesnake doesn't like the rain forest. More often than not, the reason animals prefer certain environments is that the environments help the animals meet their specific needs. For example, a whale can't live on dry land, and a parrot won't survive in the Atlantic Ocean.

With your classmates, discuss the preferred environments of the animals in the following chart. Write down key words describing that environment. Then, present your chart and key words to the class.

Animal	Preferred Environment	Key Words
Lion	Area good for hunting	Plains Open areas
Hawk		
Shark		
House cat		
Cobra		

Expanding the Paragraph

As you have learned, a paragraph consists of three parts: a topic sentence, supporting sentences (the body), and a concluding sentence. Notice these three parts in Model Paragraph 1 on page 56.

Model Paragraph 1

Man's Best Friend

topic sentence

<u>There are three main relationships that dogs have with people</u>. [First, we have working dogs. These dogs, such as Siberian huskies and collies, serve people almost like employees. To a sheep farmer, for example, a good sheepdog is his most valuable partner. Other dogs are known primarily for their excellence in sports. The sleek and supremely fast greyhound is used in dog races, and many hunting dogs, such as setters, retrievers, and pointers, often compete in hunting trials. Third, many people enjoy dogs as companions. All kinds of dogs can be excellent companions, but a few breeds are kept only for this purpose. Some examples are the toy dogs, such as a Chihuahua or a Lhasa apso.] <u>Because of the relationships they have with people, dogs are often called "man's best friend."</u>

[body]

concluding sentence

sleek: smooth and elegant **supremely**: extremely	**a hunting trial**: a competition where dogs get awards for excellent hunting behavior	**a breed**: a group of animals or plants that are similar in characteristics

When you want to write about a topic in more detail, you can turn your paragraph into an essay. Paragraphs can be easily expanded to essay length. Similar to a paragraph, an essay is also composed of three sections. These sections are an **introductory paragraph**; **supporting paragraphs,** or a **body**; and a **concluding paragraph**. Here is an essay on the same topic.

Model Essay 1

Man's Best Friend

The dog is generally considered the first domesticated animal. The domesticated dog has lived with human beings as a working partner and household pet in all eras and cultures since the time people lived in caves. It is generally believed that the direct ancestor of the domestic dog is the wolf, originally found throughout Europe, Asia, and North America. Archeologists have found remains of dogs that are 10,000 years old. In these ancient societies, as well as in our modern one, there are three main relationships that dogs have with people.

First, we have the working dogs. These dogs, such as Siberian huskies and collies, serve people almost like employees. The dogs help pull heavy loads, round up cattle, and keep a sharp eye out for strangers. To a sheep farmer, for example, a good sheepdog is his most valuable partner. Sheepdogs, such as Border collies, standard collies, and Shetland sheepdogs, are very intelligent and can learn to respond to hand signals as well as spoken words. Sheepdogs in Scotland, for instance, move sheep along with barely a glance from the shepherd. As a result, working dogs know their worth to their master, and they are proud of it.

Other dogs are known primarily for their excellence in sports. The sleek and supremely fast greyhound is used in dog races. These races take place on specially prepared tracks where the competitors chase a mechanical rabbit. People gamble on these athletes' performance. Bird dogs are a type of hunting dog. Setters and pointers, for example, recognize a bird's scent long before it makes a sound and show their owner where the bird is by standing rock still. Retrievers, such as golden retrievers or Labrador retrievers, will throw themselves into an icy cold lake to pick up the bird their owner has shot. These special hunting dogs often compete in hunting trials. Clearly, sporting dogs are the athletes of the dog world.

Third, many people enjoy a dog as a companion. All kinds of dogs can be excellent companions. Both the working dogs and the hunting dogs have great patience and are very good with small children. Most of these dogs will allow children to climb all over them and are great baby-sitters because of their loyalty to their owner and their family. A few breeds are kept only for the purpose of being a companion. Some of these are the toy dogs, such as a Chihuahua or a Lhasa apso. Since these dogs are so tiny, they are great to have if you live in a small apartment. In short, all dogs, including the toy dogs, are wonderful companions.

Although there are a great many breeds of dogs, they can be classified into these three main types by their relationships to their owners. Even if you have no interest in sports and no farm to run, you can have a great companion in a dog. Because of the relationships they have with people, dogs are often called "man's best friend."

domesticated: animals that live near people and are controlled by them	**an ancestor**: a member of your family that lived in the past	**a competitor**: someone or something trying to win
an era: a long period in history that begins with a particular date or event	**to round up**: to find and gather together a group of people or things	**mechanical**: made from or powered by equipment
		an athlete: a person who is a competitor in sports

Look at page 58 to see how a paragraph is expanded into an essay. The topic sentence of the paragraph becomes the **thesis statement** of the essay, which comes at the end of the introductory paragraph. The supporting sentences of the original paragraph expand into three separate body paragraphs in the essay. In other words, each major supporting sentence and its minor supports in Model Paragraph 1 become one body paragraph in the corresponding essay. Finally, the concluding sentence is made into a concluding paragraph.

Two other points are important to note. First, notice how each body paragraph mirrors the construction of the original paragraph. Just as the paragraphs you have written so far have had a topic sentence, supporting sentences, and a concluding sentence, so does each body paragraph. Second, notice how the body paragraphs support the thesis statement of the essay just as the supporting sentences in a paragraph support the topic sentence.

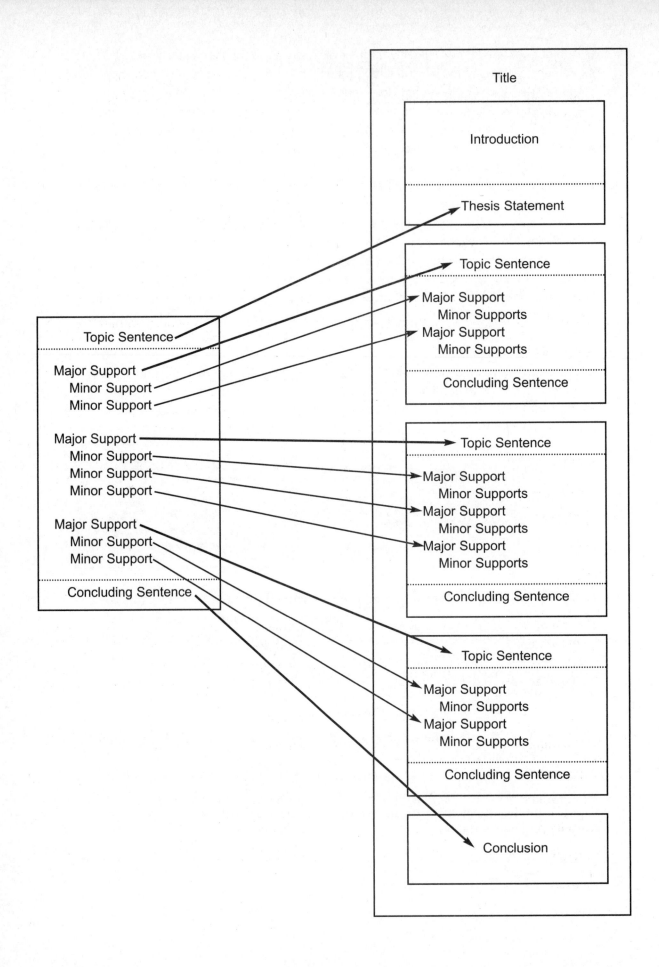

Analyze this paragraph by labeling the three main parts: topic sentence, body, and concluding sentence.

Animal Camouflage

    Many animals find security in blending in with their environment. In birds, for example, it is quite common for adult males to be brightly colored and very noticeable, while adult females and young chicks are light brown or sand colored in order to blend into their background and escape the sharp eyes of a predator. Many mammals have also adopted the colors of their surroundings over the years. A zebra is almost invisible among the branches and stripes of sunlight in its native Africa, and a lion is very hard to see when it is sleeping on the beige sand of the plains. Most fish are darker on top than on the bottom; from above, they look like the land at the bottom of the water, and from below, they look like the water's surface. The safety that these animals' protective coloring provides has helped them survive over the ages.

camouflage: hiding something by making it look the same as the things around it	**to blend in**: to mix in with, to be similar to other things **a predator**: a hunter, usually an animal	**a mammal**: a warm-blooded animal that gives birth to live babies and drinks milk from its mother's breast when it is young

▶ *Practice 2*   Analyzing an Essay

This essay is an expansion of the paragraph about animal camouflage. First, draw boxes around the three components of the essay (introductory paragraph, supporting paragraphs, and concluding paragraph). Next, using a different colored pen, underline the topic and concluding sentences in each body paragraph.

Animal Camouflage

    Animals in the wild have many natural enemies. A small bird wants to avoid being seen by a hawk, a zebra doesn't want the lion to find him, and a flatfish would prefer that the shark swim quietly by. If an animal can't easily run away from its predator, how can it protect itself? One way that has evolved over time is protective coloring, or camouflage. Many animals find security in blending in with their environment.

In birds, for example, although it is quite common for adult males to be brightly colored and very noticeable, adult females and young chicks are light brown or sand colored in order to blend into their background and escape the sharp eyes of a predator. This coloring protects the weaker birds. Consider the bright red cardinal, a very common bird in colder areas of North America. The male is like a red fire engine against white snow, but you hardly ever see the females. They are sandy brown, with touches of red on the wings, tail, and breast. The peacock is another bird where the male is bright and showy, while the female is easily overlooked because of her dull coloring. The long tail feathers of the male are generally bright green and gold and have round markings of a rich color, known as peacock blue. The female, called a peahen, has short tail feathers and is much less colorful than the male. Adopting camouflage colors helps the female birds survive and raise another generation of birds.

Many mammals have also adopted the colors of their surroundings. A zebra is almost invisible among the branches and stripes of sunlight in its native Africa because its black and white stripes mimic the shadows among the trees and bushes. A lion is very hard to see when it is sleeping on the beige sand of the plains. The lioness, in particular, looks just like a part of the ground until she raises  her head. The camouflage of the lioness makes her invisible to her prey so she can concentrate on hunting and feeding her young. All these mammals have, over many, many years, developed protective coloring to assist them in the struggle to survive.

Most fish are darker on top than on the bottom; from above, they look like the land at the bottom of the water, and from below, they look like the water's surface. Many ocean fish have a horizontal line along their body that separates the top from the bottom. An ocean mackerel, for example, is easily distinguished by this dark stripe. Some flatfish have taken this protection a step further; for example, a fish that lives on a sandy bottom has a light-brown upper side, while a flatfish that lives on a rocky bottom has an upper side that looks like pebbles. Because they look just like their surroundings, these fish survive and avoid becoming someone else's lunch.

Looking like their environment is helpful to these animals for the survival of the species. The mother bird that is invisible among the brown leaves, the lion snoozing on the sandy plains, and the fish that hides among the pebbles will live to see another day. The safety these animals find in their protective coloring has helped them survive over the ages.

---

a chick: a baby bird

dull: boring, unnoticeable, not bright or shiny

invisible: not able to be seen

to mimic: to copy the way someone or something is

prey: animal that is hunted and eaten by another animal

horizontal: flat, level, and straight; in the same direction as the horizon

a species: a category of the classification of animals or plants

to snooze: to sleep lightly for a short time

▶ *Practice 3*   Outlining an Essay

Here is part of an outline of the essay "Animal Camouflage." Complete the outline by writing in the key words from each paragraph of the essay.

I. Introductory paragraph

▶ *Thesis statement:* Many animals find security in blending in with their environment.

II. Body

A. Paragraph 1: Birds

▶ *Topic sentence:* In birds, for example, although it is quite common for adult males to be brightly colored and very noticeable, adult females and young chicks are light brown or sand colored in order to blend into their background and escape the sharp eyes of a predator.

Major support 1:

▶ _____

Minor support(s):

▶ _____
_____

Major support 2:

▶ _____

Minor support(s):

▶ _____
_____

▶ *Concluding sentence:* Adopting camouflage colors helps the female birds survive and raise another generation of birds.

▶ *Topic sentence:* Many mammals have also adopted the colors of their surroundings.

    Major support 1:

▶ _____

    Major support 2:

▶ _____

        Minor support(s):

▶ _____

    _____

▶ *Concluding sentence:* All these mammals have, over many, many years, developed protective coloring to assist them in the struggle to survive.

C. Paragraph 3: Fish

▶ *Topic sentence:* Most fish are darker on top than on the bottom; from above, they look like the land at the bottom of the water, and from below, they look like the water's surface.

    Major support 1:

▶ _____

        Minor support(s):

▶ _____

    _____

    Major support 2:

▶ _____

▶ *Concluding sentence:* Because they look just like their surroundings, these fish survive and avoid becoming someone else's lunch.

III. Concluding paragraph

Mechanics

Semicolons with Transitions

As you learned in Chapter 4, transitions are words that make connections. Look back at the chart on page 39 that lists the most common transitions.

Transitions are usually followed by a comma when they occur at the beginning of a sentence. The usual pattern is:

Independent clause. *Transition,* independent clause.

Another common pattern is to use a semicolon instead of a period. In this case, the pattern is:

Independent clause; *transition,* independent clause.

Here are a few examples of this pattern.

- Your first reason is clear; however, your second is unclear.
- It is raining today; therefore, my pet snake can't go outside.
- She tore up all her old love letters; then, she filed for divorce.

▶ *Practice 4* Punctuating with Commas and Semicolons

Punctuate these sentences. Use commas and semicolons in the appropriate places.

1. Baby whales stay with their mothers for one to two years after that they usually go out on their own.

2. Loggers in the Northwest cut down the forests consequently they destroy some animals' natural habitats.

3. First we'll feed the dogs later on we'll feed ourselves.

4. The city government is trying many ways to decrease the number of wild cats in the park for instance animal control officers are catching the cats and neutering them.

5. Furthermore the police can suspend your dog's license.

6. Frank seems to hate people on the other hand he is very loving with his cats.

7. Some birds live permanently in the Arctic however most migrate.

8. For example I never leave home without my dogs.

▶ *Writing To Communicate*

Almost everyone has moved at some point in his or her life. You may have moved from the countryside to a city, from one state or region to another, or even to a different country. As discussed in the chapter opener, the environment often plays a big role in our choice of where to live. In addition, once we move, we often make many changes based on our new environment. How did your life change when you moved?

On the following page are the introductory and concluding paragraphs of an essay and space to write, in outline form, the content of the body paragraphs. The title of this essay is "Adapting to a New Environment." The thesis of the essay is that people change their ways of behaving when they move to a new environment. Follow these steps in writing your essay:

1. Talk with your classmates about how all of you have made changes in your lives as a result of moving to a different environment. Some changes might be the way you dress, the way you speak, the way you travel (e.g., driving a car vs. using public transportation), how you look at strangers, what you do for entertainment, and so on.

2. Make a list and select three types of changes that have been true for you.

3. Next, write a topic sentence for each of those changes, and write a few examples in note form underneath each topic sentence.

4. Finally, copy the introduction, write your body paragraphs, and copy the conclusion. Use good paragraph format.

5. Share your essay with a classmate, using the Peer Help Worksheet on page 66 to help improve each other's essays.

Note: You may not need to use two major supports for every paragraph, and you may want to have more than two in other paragraphs. As the writer, you make these decisions based on what you want to say to your readers.

Adapting to a New Environment

I. Introductory paragraph

▶   Human beings are very adaptable. We can live in most climates of the world. In the past, people tended to stay in the place they were born, but now we move easily from countryside to city, from one part of a country to another, and even from country to country. Each place has its own customs and ways of life, and countries also have different languages. When I moved from _____ to _____, I changed my behavior in three significant ways.

II. Body

A. Paragraph 1

▶ *Topic sentence:* _____

_____

Major support 1:

▶ _____

   Minor support(s):

   ▶ _____

   _____

Major support 2:

▶ _____

   Minor support(s):

   ▶ _____

   _____

B. Paragraph 2

▶ *Topic sentence:* _____

_____

    Major support 1:

    ▶ _____

        Minor support(s):

        ▶ _____

        _____

    Major support 2:

    ▶ _____

        Minor support(s):

        ▶ _____

        _____

C. Paragraph 3

▶ *Topic sentence:* _____

_____

    Major support 1:

    ▶ _____

        Minor support(s):

        ▶ _____

        _____

    Major support 2:

    ▶ _____

        Minor support(s):

        ▶ _____

        _____

III. Concluding paragraph

▶   Am I the same person I was before or am I different now? Change makes us examine our values and our habits. By changing my _____ , my _____ , and my _____ , I think I may appear to others as if I am a new person. I don't really think so, however. I prefer to think of it not so much as having changed but as having grown.

Peer Help Worksheet

In Part I of this book, you used Paragraph Checklists to help you learn to revise and edit your own paragraphs. To expand this idea, you will now use your classmates, or peers, to help you improve your writing while you help them improve theirs. Read your partner's writing and comment on it, using this Peer Help Worksheet.

Peer Help Worksheet

Check off each step as you complete it.

1 Which change in your partner's essay do you think was explained most clearly? Why?

2 Organization

    a. Does each body paragraph have a topic sentence? If yes, underline the topic sentences and circle the controlling ideas. If no, make a suggestion of an appropriate topic sentence. .... ❏

    b. Does each paragraph have sufficient support, in your view? If not, explain why. .... ❏

3 Editing

    a. Has each paragraph been indented? .... ❏

    b. What transitions are used in the essay? List them here. _____ .... ❏

    c. Are all the commas, semicolons, and periods used with the transitions correct? Circle any that you think need to be changed. .... ❏

CHAPTER 7 ▶ The Thesis Statement

How Human Beings Shape Their Environment

Almost everything we do has an effect on the environment. Ask three classmates questions about the changes that have occurred in their countries or in countries they know about.

Discuss the four environmental areas in the chart below. Fill in the chart with a few key words from their answers. For example, you might find that in some parts of Mexico, the air pollution problem keeps getting worse because of the rapid growth of the cities. After you have filled in the chart, discuss with your classmates whether different countries have similar concerns.

	Name: Country: Continent:	Name: Country: Continent:	Name: Country: Continent:
1. Water supply			
2. Forests			
3. Air			
4. Animals			

Parts of a Thesis Statement

The **thesis statement** is the most important sentence in your essay. It is the main idea for the whole essay, and it frequently shows (directly or indirectly) the number and the content of the body paragraphs of the essay. Clear thesis statements are essential for good essay writing in English.

Topic and Controlling Idea

A thesis statement has two main parts: the topic and the controlling idea. The **topic** is the subject of the essay, what the essay is about. The **controlling idea** is what you are going to say about the topic. As you can see, the thesis statement of an essay is made up of the same parts as the topic sentence in a paragraph. This is because the thesis statement in an essay has the same function as the topic sentence in a paragraph.

Below are the thesis statements from the two essays in Chapter 6 on pages 56 and 59. The topics have been underlined and the controlling ideas have been circled.

There are (three main) relationships that dogs have with people.

Many animals (find security in blending in with their environment.)

As with topic sentences, it is not enough to just state the topic of the essay in the thesis statement. You must also tell the reader what your essay will say about the topic, which means that you need to have a controlling idea. Naturally, for any one topic there are many possibilities for controlling ideas. For example, with the topic *dogs*, you could write thesis statements such as:

Since they were first domesticated, dogs (have helped human beings a lot.)

In this essay, you would give examples of how dogs can be helpful to people.

There are (many types of) dogs.

In this essay, you would discuss the various types of dogs.

An English setter and a Gordon setter have (a few obvious differences, but they) (are mostly similar.)

In this essay, you would describe the differences and similarities between two breeds of dogs: an English setter and a Gordon setter.

Predictor

In addition, some thesis statements may also have a third component called a predictor. The **predictor** of a thesis statement tells the reader how many body paragraphs there will be in the essay and what their content will be. For example:

Wars in the twentieth century were fought for three main reasons: ethnic, economic, and religious.

In this thesis statement, the topic is *wars in the twentieth century*. The controlling idea is that they *were fought for three reasons*. The third part of this thesis statement lists the three reasons that the author believes were most important: *ethnic* reasons, *economic* reasons, and *religious* reasons. We call this third part of the thesis statement the predictor because it predicts the number and content of the essay paragraphs.

Look at these thesis statements. The topics of the statements are underlined, the controlling ideas are circled, and the predictors are boxed.

1. <u>Living in a city</u> (is more exciting) than <u>living in the suburbs</u> because of the many people, the variety of things to buy, and the fun places to go.

2. Discrimination, lack of economic opportunity, and inferior education are the (three main) <u>causes of poverty</u> today.

▶ *Practice 1*   Identifying the Parts of Thesis Statements

Read these four thesis statements and answer the questions.

1. Modern methods of building houses have greatly increased their ability to withstand earthquakes.

   What is the topic? _____

   What is the controlling idea? _____

   If there is a predictor, what is it? _____

2. Its beauty, history, and location make Washington, D.C., a fascinating place to visit.

   What is the topic? _____

   What is the controlling idea? _____

   If there is a predictor, what is it? _____

3. There is considerable evidence to show that there is life on other planets.

   What is the topic? _____

   What is the controlling idea? _____

   If there is a predictor, what is it? _____

4. Three characteristics of the houses in my country show that it gets very cold there in winter: the thick walls, the two-door entries, and the steep roofs.

   What is the topic? _____

   What is the controlling idea? _____

   If there is a predictor, what is it? _____

▶ *Practice 2* Predicting Essay Content

Predict the content of the body paragraphs from these three thesis statements. Write two or three key words describing the content of the body paragraphs that you think will follow each thesis statement.

1. As we human beings shape our environment by building and producing, we are increasingly polluting our air, our water, and our soil.

    Body paragraph 1: _____

    Body paragraph 2: _____

    Body paragraph 3: _____

2. The main advantages of urban planning are that we can control a city's appearance, we can organize transportation effectively, and we can make sure there are enough open spaces.

    Body paragraph 1: _____

    Body paragraph 2: _____

    Body paragraph 3: _____

3. With its winding paths, lakes, and small forests, Central Park in New York City is the most important example of the romantic style of landscape architecture in the United States.

    Body paragraph 1: _____

    Body paragraph 2: _____

    Body paragraph 3: _____

Rules for Thesis Statements

1. A thesis statement must be a *statement*, not a question.

Not a thesis statement:	Are dogs good companions?
Thesis statement:	Dogs are good companions.

2. A thesis statement must be a *complete sentence*. This means that it must have a subject and a verb with a tense.

Not a thesis statement:	City living hazardous to your health.
Thesis statement:	City living is hazardous to your health.

3. A thesis statement is an *opinion*; it cannot be a simple statement of fact. A fact does not need any support, and therefore you cannot write an essay about it.

| *Not a thesis statement:* | I have an older brother and a younger brother. |
| *Thesis statement:* | I have much more in common with my younger brother than I do with my older brother. |

4. A thesis statement must *state* the controlling idea. This means that you must state your position on the topic; you cannot simply announce the topic of your essay.

| *Not a thesis statement:* | This essay is about air pollution. |
| *Thesis statement:* | Recent methods of reducing air pollution are showing some positive results. |

5. A thesis statement should have only *one* controlling idea.

| *Not a thesis statement:* | Public transportation in my hometown is too expensive, and it is slower than the transportation in Tokyo. |
| *Thesis statement:* | Public transportation in my hometown is too expensive. |

▶ *Practice 3* Thesis Statements

Put a check mark in front of the sentences that are thesis statements. If a sentence is *not* a thesis statement, write the number(s) of the rule(s) it violates on the line in front of it, and change it so that it is a thesis statement.

_____ 1. Japanese cars are better than American cars.

_____ 2. A Mitsubishi is a Japanese car.

_____ 3. I'm going to show you why seat belts are necessary.

_____ 4. Are seat belts necessary?

_____ 5. Wearing a seat belt can save your life.

_____ 6. Students who work while they are studying meet a lot of people, and their professors also work hard.

_____ 7. There are both advantages and disadvantages to working while you are an undergraduate.

_____ 8. Work–study programs have more advantages than disadvantages.

_____ 9. Work–study programs: an analysis.

_____ 10. In this essay, I will compare working on campus and working off campus.

▶ *Practice 4* Writing Thesis Statements

Choose five of these eight topics and write a good thesis statement for each. At least three of your five statements should have a predictor.

Example

More and more species of animals are becoming endangered because of pollution, excessive hunting, and expanding industry.

1. Wild animals
2. Endangered species
3. Forests/vegetation
4. Transportation

5. The world's changing climate
6. Oceans/water
7. The world's food production
8. Housing

Mechanics

Comma Splices

A common punctuation problem is a comma splice. A **comma splice** is an error that occurs when a comma by itself is used between two independent clauses. A comma is correct between two independent clauses, but only when it is followed by a coordinating conjunction. Look at this example sentence with a comma splice:

> My dad hung a bird feeder in the backyard, he loves to watch the birds eat from it.

There are four common ways to correct comma splices:

1. Put a period in the place of the comma and capitalize the first word of the next sentence.

   > My dad hung a bird feeder in the backyard. He loves to watch the birds eat from it.

2. Put a semicolon in the place of the comma.

   > My dad hung a bird feeder in the backyard; he loves to watch the birds eat from it.

3. Insert a coordinating conjunction. (See Chapter 3.)

   > My dad hung a bird feeder in the backyard, and he loves to watch the birds eat from it.

4. Change one of the clauses into a dependent clause by starting it with a subordinating conjunction. (See Chapter 4.)

   > Since my dad hung a bird feeder in the backyard, he loves to watch the birds eat from it.

► *Practice 5* **Correcting Comma Splices**

This paragraph has four comma splices. Find them and correct them. Try to use each of the four ways explained on page 72.

Planting Roses

Planting roses is easy if you follow these steps. First you need to measure the diameter of the roots, next you must dig a hole twice as big as that diameter. This hole should be so deep that the roots have plenty of room to grow. Mix some rose fertilizer with the soil at the bottom of the hole, this is to help the rose to flower later. The next step is to form a little hill in the middle of the hole, you are going to spread out the roots over the top of this hill. Hold the rose firmly with one hand and spread out the roots with your other hand. Be careful not to break the roots, they are quite delicate. While you are holding the plant with one hand, pat the soil down gently around the roots. Continue putting soil over the roots until the area around the plant is filled up to a level a little lower than the soil level around it. Finally, water your plant thoroughly. With enough water and some sunshine, you should see your rose plant begin to grow leaves in a few weeks.

Run-on Sentences

Another common punctuation problem is a run-on sentence. In **run-on sentences**, two or more independent clauses follow each other without any punctuation. Look at this example of a run-on sentence:

> Cutting down the rain forests leads to the extinction of plants and animals their habitats are destroyed.

There are three common ways to correct run-on sentences:

1. Make two separate sentences.

   > Cutting down the rain forests leads to the extinction of plants and animals. Their habitats are destroyed.

2. Add extra words.

   > When their habitats are destroyed due to cutting down the rain forests, many plants and animals become extinct.

3. Add a subordinating conjunction.

   > Cutting down the rain forests leads to the extinction of plants and animals because their habitats are destroyed.

▶ Practice 6 Adding Necessary Punctuation

The following paragraph has no punctuation. Correct it by adding capital letters, commas, semicolons, and periods. (*Hint:* There are six complete sentences in the paragraph.)

City Growth

Cities can grow in an organic way or in a planned way organic cities are usually older cities they are called organic because they have spread in different directions with no precise plan except to accommodate the growing population on the other hand the modern planned cities are sometimes designed before they are even really established in a such a plan careful attention is paid to the amount of residential and commercial spaces in short there are two types of city growth.

▶ Writing To Communicate

In this section, you will generate ideas, organize those ideas, and write the body paragraphs for an essay where the thesis statement is given.

Generating Ideas

In Chapter 2 on page 11, you learned that there are two common ways of generating ideas: brainstorming and freewriting. In this section, you will brainstorm possible examples, facts, or illustrations that can be used to support a thesis statement. One way to brainstorm is to use a circle diagram. First, draw a circle on a piece of paper and write the topic of discussion in the center of the circle. Then, draw lines out from the circle and write down different things about that topic. From each line, draw other branching lines and write key words of examples or facts that demonstrate that area of thesis support. The lines coming out from the circle directly will be the topics of the body paragraphs, and the branching lines coming off these topic lines will be the major supports of the body paragraphs. In most cases, your brainstorming will generate a few topic lines from the circle that you later discard as irrelevant.

Look at this sample thesis statement:

The system of public transportation in this town is awful.

The lines coming out from the circle support the thesis statement, and the branching lines support the major points. In this example, there isn't a predictor, so you need to determine which topics for the body paragraphs best support the controlling idea ("awful") of the thesis statement.

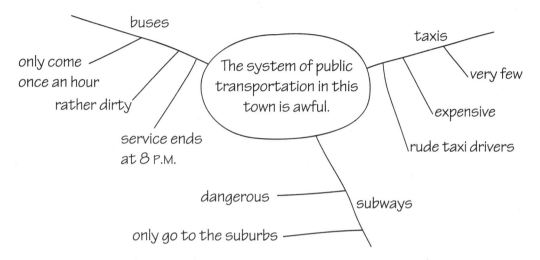

Choose a thesis statement that you wrote in Practice 4 on page 72, and write it in the circle. Then draw lines from it that will become major supports in the essay. Add ideas from the brainstorming to the lines by drawing branching lines for the supporting points.

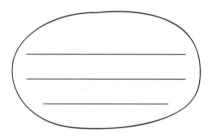

Organizing Ideas

Now that you have brainstormed ideas to support the thesis statement, use this outline to organize your ideas. Write your topic sentences for the body paragraphs and the supporting points that you want to use.

Body Paragraph 1

▶ *Topic sentence 1:* _____

_____

      <u>Support 1:</u> _____

      <u>Support 2:</u> _____

      <u>Support 3:</u> _____

<u>Body paragraph 2</u>

▶ *Topic sentence 2:* _____

_____

<u>Support 1:</u> _____

<u>Support 2:</u> _____

<u>Support 3:</u> _____

<u>Body paragraph 3</u>

▶ *Topic sentence 3:* _____

_____

<u>Support 1:</u> _____

<u>Support 2:</u> _____

<u>Support 3:</u> _____

Writing a First Draft

Now, work on this essay. Write your thesis statement as a separate one-sentence paragraph and add two or three body paragraphs, following your outline. Give your essay a title. Be sure to use correct paragraph format. (Note that this essay will not be a complete essay because it does not have an introductory paragraph and a concluding paragraph.)

Peer Help Worksheet

Check off each step as you complete it.

1 What did you learn from your partner's essay?

2 Organization

    a. Does each body paragraph have a topic sentence? .... ☐

    b. Does each body paragraph support the thesis statement? ..... ☐

    c. Is each paragraph unified? Underline any sentences that you think are irrelevant. .... ☐

3 Editing

    a. Are all the verb tenses correct? Circle any that you think need to be changed. .... ☐

    b. Are there any comma splices or run-on sentences? .... ☐

CHAPTER 8　The Introductory Paragraph

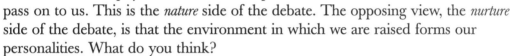

Nature vs. Nurture

The writing theme in this chapter explores a long-standing debate among scientists concerning the origin of personality traits. Some people think that we are born with our personalities just as we are born with the physical traits that our parents pass on to us. This is the *nature* side of the debate. The opposing view, the *nurture* side of the debate, is that the environment in which we are raised forms our personalities. What do you think?

Read each of the following five pairs of statements that describe personality traits. Choose the statement from each pair that best describes you. Then, check one of the boxes to indicate whether you think you have inherited this trait from your parents (nature) or from something or someone in your environment (nurture).

Intelligence

❏ I am more artistic than academic.
❏ I am more academic than artistic.

This trait comes from

❏ one of my parents.
❏ my environment.

*　*　*

Interests

❏ I would rather read than play sports.
❏ I would rather play sports than read.

This trait comes from

❏ one of my parents.
❏ my environment.

*　*　*

Motivation

❏ Success is more important to me than relationships.
❏ Relationships are more important to me than success.

This trait comes from

❏ one of my parents.

❏ my environment.

*　*　*

Outlook

❏ I am generally optimistic about the future.
❏ I am generally pessimistic about the future.

This trait comes from

❏ one of my parents.
❏ my environment.

*　*　*

Relationships

❏ I prefer to work in groups.
❏ I prefer to work alone.

This trait comes from

❏ one of my parents.
❏ my environment.

How do your answers compare to your classmates' answers? Do your answers vary according to the trait? Does culture play a role?

Guidelines for Introductory Paragraphs

The first paragraph in an essay is called the **introductory paragraph**. Without an introductory paragraph, your essay may start too abruptly. You need to lead readers to the subject of the essay in an interesting way and show them that reading your essay is worth their time. As a result, the purpose of the introductory paragraph is twofold: to get the readers' attention and to introduce the subject of the essay to them—in that order.

There are several guidelines for writing a good introductory paragraph.

- It must be relevant to the topic; that is, it should not introduce material not covered in the essay.

- It should not preview the points that will form the body of the essay.

- There should be at least two sentences before the thesis statement. In other words, the introductory paragraph should be a minimum of three sentences.

- The thesis statement should come at the end of the introductory paragraph.

Types of Introductory Paragraphs

There are many ways for a writer to get the readers' attention in an introductory paragraph. Four of the most common ways are discussed here.

Anecdote

An **anecdote** is a brief story that illustrates your topic. You can either base this anecdote on your own experience or invent a story about someone else. Model Paragraph 1 is an example of a personal anecdote, while Model Paragraph 2 demonstrates the use of a third-person anecdote.

Model Paragraph 1

My younger brother was a good student until our parents got divorced. Then, while my parents' lives became a war zone over property and emotions, my brother withdrew into himself and felt abandoned and unloved. He needed to feel that he was a part of something. That's when he got involved with a gang at his high school. The gang he joined became his family and was more important to him than anything. My parents didn't notice until my brother got badly hurt in a gang fight. I am convinced that *gangs are a direct result of the breakdown of the traditional family*.

What About You?

Gang is a word that is used for a group of young people who usually cause trouble. Are gangs common in your country? How do you feel about gangs?

Model Paragraph 2

The teenager hated to be at home. His parents were always fighting—at least on the rare occasions that both of them were at home at the same time. His mother was on drugs, and his father was an alcoholic. He felt totally alone at home, but when he was with his fellow gang members, he felt as if he belonged. He loved being with the members of his gang and would do anything for them and with them. This all-too-common example illustrates why I think that *gangs are a direct result of the breakdown of the traditional family*.

Interesting Facts or Statistics

Another way to introduce your essay is with **interesting facts** or **statistics**. To write this kind of introduction, you need to be aware of commonly known information. You can expand your knowledge of facts and statistics by carefully reading newspapers and journals. Here is an example of an introductory paragraph using facts and statistics.

Model Paragraph 3

It is estimated that there are nearly 5,000 gangs in the United States with a total of almost 250,000 members. In fact, in inner cities, where gangs are most common, 7 percent of all teenagers are gang members. Why are all these young adults choosing to be gang members? In my opinion, *gangs are a direct result of the breakdown of the traditional family*.

Historical Introduction

You may also choose to write a brief **historical introduction** to your essay. Naturally, this is not meant to be a comprehensive account; it simply provides general historical background.

Model Paragraph 4

Gangs have existed in the United States for at least 100 years. At the turn of the twentieth century, there were many gangs in big East Coast cities. These gangs were mostly made up of members of the same ethnic group and primarily protected the neighborhood where their families lived. Nowadays, however, gang members have little to do with protecting their relatives. It's my belief that *gangs are a direct result of the breakdown of the traditional family*.

General to Specific

This is perhaps the most common type of introduction. It begins with a **general** statement of the larger topic, and then each sentence narrows it down until you get to the **specific** thesis statement. The trick is to start out general, but not too general. Remember to keep the introduction relevant. Here is an example of a general-to-specific introduction.

Model Paragraph 5

It's difficult to grow up in this society. A teenager can get into all kinds of trouble with school, smoking, drugs, and dating. One of the worst kinds of trouble that a teenager can get into is getting involved with a gang. Gang members commit crimes and get hurt or killed all too often. Why do teenagers get involved in gangs? I think that *gangs are a direct result of the breakdown of the traditional family.*

As you can see, any of the above paragraphs could introduce an essay about the reasons gangs exist. In your essays, try to develop the skill of writing different types of introductions, so your essays do not become boring and predictable.

▶ Practice 1   Evaluating Introductory Paragraphs

Read the thesis statement and the four introductory paragraphs that follow. Decide whether or not each paragraph is a good introductory paragraph. If it is, check off which kind of introduction it is. If it isn't, check off the reason(s) why it isn't. Look back to page 78 if you need help.

Thesis statement: Heredity plays a more important role in a child's personality development than environment does.

1. A man meets a woman, and they fall in love. Then, they get married, buy a house, and settle down. After a while, they decide to have children. The woman gets pregnant, and nine months later a baby is born. In this case, *heredity plays a more important role in a child's personality development than environment does.*

    a. Is this a good introductory paragraph?
        ❏ Yes   ❏ No

    b. If it is good, which kind of introduction is it?
        ❏ Anecdote (personal or third person)   ❏ Historical
        ❏ Facts and/or statistics   ❏ General to specific

    c. If it isn't good, check off why.
        ❏ Some content not relevant to   ❏ Too short
           thesis statement
        ❏ Previews content of the body   ❏ Too general

2. As you will see below, there are lots of studies of twins and of adopted children that indicate that genes are important in a child's development. When twins who were separated at birth are reunited in adulthood, they find many likes and dislikes in common. Also, when adopted children are reunited with their

biological parents, they often find many similar personality attributes. I believe that *heredity plays a more important role in a child's personality development than environment does.*

    a. Is this a good introductory paragraph?
        ❐ Yes   ❐ No

    b. If it is good, which kind of introduction is it?
        ❐ Anecdote (personal or third person)   ❐ Historical
        ❐ Facts and/or statistics   ❐ General to specific

    c. If it isn't good, check off why.
        ❐ Some content not relevant to   ❐ Too short
            thesis statement
        ❐ Previews content of the body   ❐ Too general

3.   I witnessed a child's birth recently and began thinking about what kind of person she would become. Would she be kind or cruel, generally happy or chronically depressed, a giver or a taker? I can predict that she will be a kind, generally happy giver because that's the way her sister is, despite her abusive parents. I also believe that *heredity plays a more important role in a child's personality development than environment does.*

    a. Is this a good introductory paragraph?
        ❐ Yes   ❐ No

    b. If it is good, which kind of introduction is it?
        ❐ Anecdote (personal or third person)   ❐ Historical
        ❐ Facts and/or statistics   ❐ General to specific

    c. If it isn't good, check off why.
        ❐ Some content not relevant to   ❐ Too short
            thesis statement
        ❐ Previews content of the body   ❐ Too general

4.   Many people think that the environment that a child is raised in is important. I think *heredity plays a more important role in a child's personality development than environment does.*

    a. Is this a good introductory paragraph?
        ❐ Yes   ❐ No

    b. If it is good, which kind of introduction is it?
        ❐ Anecdote (personal or third person)   ❐ Historical
        ❐ Facts and/or statistics   ❐ General to specific

    c. If it isn't good, check off why.
        ❐ Some content not relevant to   ❐ Too short
            thesis statement
        ❐ Previews content of the body   ❐ Too general

► **Practice 2** Writing an Introductory Paragraph Using Statistics

The following chart shows the number of Americans who have died in several wars. Write an introductory paragraph for the thesis statement using the statistics from the table. Remember that the thesis statement goes at the end of the introductory paragraph.

Thesis statement: The three basic causes for the participation of the United States in wars have been economic, ideological, and defensive.

War (U.S. Involvement)	Total Number of U.S. Soldiers	Number of Combat Deaths	Percentage of Soldiers Who Died
Revolutionary War (1775–1783)	250,000	6,824	2.7
Civil War (1861–1865)	2,213,363	140,414	6.3
World War I (1914–1918)	4,743,825	53,513	0.1
World War II (1941–1945)	16,353,659	292,131	1.7
Korean War (1950–1953)	5,764,143	33,629	0.9
Vietnam War (1961–1973)	8,744,000	47,321	0.5
Gulf War (1991)	500,000	149	<0.01

► **Practice 3** Writing Different Introductory Paragraphs

Choose one of the thesis statements below. Then write at least two introductory paragraphs for it. Remember that you can introduce a thesis statement by the use of anecdotes (personal or third person), interesting facts or statistics, historical information, or going from general ideas to specific ones.

1. Washington, D.C., is an interesting place to visit. (You can also use another city.)

2. Three experiences (childhood, frightening, or exciting) have changed my life.

3. Educational toys are better than toys that are just made to be fun.

4. Evolution (or Creationism) best explains the origin of human beings.

5. Graffiti can be art.

Mechanics

Using Commas: Lists

In English writing, commas are usually used between all words in a list of more than two items. The items can be of any grammatical structure, and the comma before the coordinating conjunction is optional. For example:

- There are three kinds of teachers: good, bad, and indifferent. (adjectives)

- Would you like coffee, tea, or a soft drink? (nouns)

- Henry got home, kissed his wife, got a beer and sat down to watch the game. (verbs)

- Jumping, skipping and hopping are what little children do best. (gerunds)

There is one further point to note about this comma pattern. If we put two or more adjectives before a noun, we often omit the coordinating conjunction.

Example

A big, blue, scary whale swam alongside our boat for several miles.

OR

A big, blue, and scary whale swam alongside our boat for several miles.

▶ Practice 4   Adding Commas to Sentences with Lists

Add commas to these sentences. Then, identify the grammatical structure in each list.

1. The suspect was messy, smelly, and half-dead.   _____adjectives_____

2. I'm not sure if our boss went to Bali Fiji or Tahiti on vacation.

   _____

3. Across the street behind the house and under the picnic table, you'll find the last Easter egg. _____

4. The team played hard made lots of points but lost the game.

   _____

5. Jill Jackson Louis Dana and I ate three pizzas last night.

   _____

6. Jen bought a big floppy blue hat on 18th Street. _____

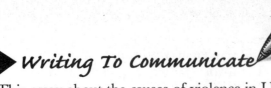

▶ Writing To Communicate

This essay about the causes of violence in U.S. society does not have an introductory paragraph. Read the essay and then write an appropriate introductory paragraph with a good thesis statement.

Violence: Nature or Nurture?

_____

_____

_____

_____

_____

_____

First of all, it's obvious that people become violent when they are trying to protect someone or something. An obvious example of this is when gang members want to protect their neighborhoods from the "invasion" of members of other gangs. However, even people who have never shown any violent tendencies might also commit a violent crime if a loved one is in danger. It is not in their nature to commit violence, but the circumstances (or environment) are causing the violence. In short, when a situation is threatening, not only gang members but also average people can act violently.

It's clear, too, that in an environment where guns are readily available, more violent crimes are committed. When you compare the United States with any country that does not allow its citizens to own guns, you will see that this is true. In a volatile situation, it's easier to reach for the gun to make your point than to continue arguing. Again, this type of environment leads to violence in people not prone to violence; that is, the tendency to violence doesn't come from the genes that a person has.

Most importantly, some people have been raised without a sense of respect for other people. They place little value on a human life. Indeed, you sometimes hear today that children want to kill someone just to know what it feels like. This is also environmental. Parents and schools can create environments where children are taught that they should respect other people, or not. How children perceive other people's rights depends on the type of situation in which they are raised.

In short, I believe that people are not born violent. They are not born with genes that make them violent. It's the environment that they are born _into_ and the situations that they find themselves in that cause them to become violent.

a tendency: a likelihood	**volatile:** quickly changing	**to be prone to:** to be likely to do something

Peer Help Worksheet

Check off each step as you complete it.

1 What caught your attention in this introductory paragraph? What made it interesting to read?

2 The type of introductory paragraph is:
(Check one.)

Personal anecdote . . . . ❑

Third-person anecdote . . . . ❑

Interesting facts or statistics . . . . ❑

Historical introduction . . . . ❑

General to specific . . . . ❑

3 Underline the thesis statement.

a. Is the thesis statement at the end of the introductory
paragraph? . . . . ❑

b. Is this introductory paragraph relevant to the thesis statement? . . ❑

c. Does the introductory paragraph avoid previewing points that
form the body of the essay? . . . . ❑

d. Are there at least two sentences before the thesis statement? . . . . ❑

e. Is the introductory paragraph too general? . . . . ❑

4 Reread the essay and note all the commas.

a. Are they used correctly? Circle any that you think might
be incorrect. . . . . ❑

b. Are there any places that you think need a comma?
Put a circle with a *C* inside it in places that you think
need a comma. . . . . ❑

CHAPTER 9 The Concluding Paragraph

▶

A Safe Environment

Look again at the meaning of the word *ecology*. It is defined as "the relationship between organisms and their environment." You are an example of an organism, and the place where you are is an example of an environment. You, of course, want to feel safe and comfortable in your environment. What do you need to feel safe? What do you need to feel comfortable? With a classmate, add two or three items in each box in the chart.

Things I Need to Feel Safe	Things I Need to Feel Comfortable
• shelter • a lock on the door	• a soft bed • coffee in the morning

Now think about when you feel uncomfortable or unsafe in an environment. Do you ever feel that you are in danger? Make a list of these things as well.

What Makes Me Feel Uncomfortable	What Makes Me Feel Unsafe	What Makes Me Feel in Danger
• crowds • too much noise	• the brake light flashing in my car • a phone call in the middle of the night	• walking alone in the dark • flying

In your country, how does the state of the natural environment affect your personal safety? In other words, if your *natural* environment (e.g., the air and the water) is clean, do you feel safe? If your natural environment is polluted, do you feel in danger?

Parts of a Concluding Paragraph

The last paragraph of your essay is, of course, the concluding paragraph. This paragraph has a very important function in your essay. Since it is the last paragraph to be read, you want your reader to leave with a clear understanding of what the point of your essay is.

A concluding paragraph consists of a summary of the points made in your body paragraphs, a restatement of the thesis statement, or a final comment on your topic. You may choose one of these ways to end your essay, or you may choose two or three. The choice is yours as the writer.

A concluding paragraph should never introduce new information about the topic of the essay. New information should go in another body paragraph, not in a concluding paragraph.

Summary

One way to end your essay is to **summarize** the main points in it. Read the following essay about homeless people. Notice the concluding paragraph.

Model Essay 1

Feeling Secure—Even without a Home

When you walk downtown in almost any large American city, you see many homeless people. They sit on the streets with their shopping carts full of their meager belongings and often ask for money. Do they make you nervous? Do they even scare you? The truth is that most homeless people do not want to be homeless, and they are afraid of the same things that you are. Homeless people, like everyone else, need basically three things to feel safe in their environment.

First, and most importantly, homeless people need to feel physical safety. For you and me, this feeling comes when we enter our apartment or house and lock the door behind us. For a homeless person, this feeling is a luxury. They may go to a shelter at night, but sometimes the people in the shelter can be dangerous, especially if they are mentally ill. Then, in the morning, they are kicked out of the shelter and forced to roam the streets. For these reasons, a lot of homeless people claim a certain bench or street corner as their own. They are trying to feel physically secure.

Second, homeless people need to have a dependable source of food. This is such a basic need that most of us don't even think about it, but for a homeless person, finding food can be a full-time job. There are places to go for meals that are usually run by local governments or churches, but there isn't enough food for everyone to have three nutritionally balanced meals a day. Getting one meal a day is considered good for a homeless person. Other food comes from scrounging through garbage or begging on the streets. It's difficult to feel secure in your environment when you don't know where your next meal is coming from.

Finally, to feel safe, you need to know that if you get sick or injure yourself, you can get the medical treatment you need. In the United States, this is becoming increasingly difficult even for people who do have places to live but don't have a lot of money. It's almost impossible

> ## What About You?
>
> Are there homeless people in your country? What does the government do to help people who don't have homes?

for a homeless person. It's true that homeless people can usually go to an emergency room in a hospital if they are gravely sick or injured, but some hospitals these days are turning away anyone who doesn't have health insurance. If the sickness or injury is not severe, there are some clinics for homeless people, but, again, the need far exceeds the availability.

In summary, the need to feel physically safe, the need for a dependable food source, and the need for medical care when necessary are essential for all of us. The constant struggle to obtain these is why homeless people do not feel secure in their environment.

meager: a little bit	**to be kicked out of**: to be told to leave	**to scrounge**: to carefully look for something, such as food or supplies
a shelter: a place where homeless people can sleep for a night	**to roam**: to walk around without direction	**gravely**: seriously
		to exceed: to go beyond

As you can see, the concluding paragraph in this essay mentions all the main ideas brought out in each of the supporting paragraphs of the essay. When you write a **summary** as a concluding paragraph, you must make sure that you include all the topics in the body paragraphs.

Restatement

An alternative to a summary is a **restatement** of the idea of your thesis statement. Here is another concluding paragraph for the essay on homeless people.

Model Paragraph 1

In short, all people want to feel safe in their environment, and to do so requires that you have these three things. These are so easy to obtain that most of us take them for granted. However, if you're homeless, getting the basics becomes more difficult and sometimes impossible.

Final Comment

Often, a concluding paragraph is most effective when you add a **final comment** to a summary or a restatement or both. Look at yet another alternative to the original concluding paragraph for the essay on homeless people.

Model Paragraph 2

In conclusion, the next time you see homeless people, try to look beyond your fear and think about how insecure they must feel in their environment. They may not know where they can go that night to feel safe or what their next meal will be. They may be worried about getting sick, or they may already be sick and have no place to go. For them, life in this world is a day-to-day struggle to survive.

▶ *Practice 1* Evaluating Concluding Paragraphs

The following essay does not have a concluding paragraph. Read the essay and the three possible concluding paragraphs that follow. Choose the best one, and be prepared to explain your choice.

The Small Strengths of Nature

We often think, and rightly so, that human beings are destroying the environment. However, it is also true that sometimes the Earth and the environment become the destroyers. Earthquakes, hurricanes, and droughts cause huge damage to vast areas of the Earth. However, on a far less extreme scale, nature is always demonstrating to us that it is stronger than we are.

For example, we cut down trees and construct houses, office and apartment buildings, roads, and sidewalks. Then, we plant other trees just where we want them so that our landscaping will be perfect. Over the years, the trees slowly–almost unnoticeably–grow taller, and their roots grow deeper, and, suddenly, our nice roads and sidewalks get cracks in them. We think that we are strong, but those trees are stronger.

Another example of nature demonstrating its power is when the small creatures of the world come into our nicely constructed environments and either destroy them or make them very unpleasant to live in. These small creatures are, of course, insects, which are far stronger than any human being. Termites can totally destroy a house, and an invasion of ants in our food can make life miserable. Indeed, the cockroaches in our cupboard have ancestors that go back millions and millions of years. How can we possibly expect to control them? In short, it's clear that insects are stronger than humans.

Even on a microscopic level, we are at the mercy of the environment. Our bodies and our scientists have developed ways of fighting the many bacteria and viruses that cause serious diseases and death. Nevertheless, there is still no cure for the common cold. We may develop vaccines and antibiotics to protect us from many viruses and bacteria, but they can change and become resistant to our attempts to destroy them. In other words, they are often stronger than we are.

Concluding Paragraphs

1. In short, we live in a world that is stronger than we are. Trees will win any long-term battle over concrete, and termites can eat buildings. I hope that this means that we will not eventually kill the Earth.

2. In conclusion, I find these small examples of nature's being stronger than humans somewhat comforting. While we attempt to control and thereby destroy our environment, the environment keeps renewing itself in small ways. Humans as a species may not survive, but I believe the Earth will.

3. All in all, nature is strong. In fact, it demonstrates this to us every day with its plants, insects, microscopic life, and weather. Isn't it time we pay attention to this fact and stop trying to control it?

What About You?

Can you think of other ways in which nature is stronger than human beings?

Mechanics

Comma Review

Look again at the uses of the comma that we have discussed in earlier chapters.

- Commas and coordinating conjunctions (Chapter 3)
- Commas and transitions (Chapter 4)
- Commas and adverbial clauses (Chapter 4)
- Commas in lists (Chapter 8)

▶ *Practice 2*   **Correcting Comma Errors**

There are four comma errors in the following paragraph. The other four uses of commas are correct. If the comma is correct, write *correct* **on the line next to the text. If there is a comma error, write** *incorrect*. **Then, correct the error by either crossing out the wrong comma or by inserting a missing comma. Some of the lines will be left blank.**

Example

Incorrect   Because snakes are cold-blooded they need the sun's heat to stay warm.

Correct   Because snakes are cold-blooded, they need the sun's heat to stay warm.

How Snakes Stay Warm

_____   Human beings are considered warm-blooded, but

_____   snakes and other reptiles are often called *cold-blooded*.

_____   This is actually not correct, because some reptiles

_____   maintain their bodies at a higher temperature than

_____   most mammals. However we use the term *cold-blooded*

_____   to refer to the fact that most reptiles rely solely on

_____   external sources of heat. Reptiles regulate their body

_____   temperatures by taking advantage of different sources

_____   of outside warmth, such as direct sunlight warm stones

_____   and the heated Earth. Because they use such heat

_____   sources to varying degrees, individual species of

_____   reptiles are able to regulate their body temperature.

_____   This body temperature may be above the temperature

_____   of the surrounding air but when the animal is inactive,

_____   the body temperature is approximately the same as

_____   that of the environment.

Writing To Communicate

This essay does not have a concluding paragraph. On a separate piece of paper write two concluding paragraphs—one with a summary and a final comment, and the other with a restatement and a final comment.

Pollution: Looking Back and Going Ahead

As we begin a new century, it might be a good idea to look back and see where we've been. Human beings accomplished a tremendous amount in the twentieth century, as the advances in medicine, technology, and the quality of life can attest. However, we often made these advances at the expense of our Mother Earth. In fact, we face the very real possibility of dying out as a species because of the damage we caused to the environment in the twentieth century. As the century closed, we were beginning to make progress in preventing the pollution of our air, water, and land, but there is still a long way to go.

In the United States, air pollution was at its worst in the 1960s. In some urban environments, it was difficult to breathe on a hot summer's day when many cars were on the road and many factories were releasing their toxic waste directly into the air. Then, in 1970, the Clean Air Act was passed by Congress, and the Environmental Protection Agency was given the authority to enforce safe standards for car and factory emissions. Since then, the air quality in many American cities has become noticeably better. Other countries also established standards, and several international agreements were made. However, there are still too many cars on the road. In developing countries especially, it is difficult to choose to protect the environment when people need jobs, so factories continue to pollute the air.

Water pollution is also a grave concern. People cannot live without water, but over the years it has been contaminated by human and animal waste, chemical runoff from factories, and even oil spills. Drinking or bathing in such polluted water causes illness and even death in many people. As early as 1956, Congress realized the necessity of establishing laws to protect our water, and the laws were subsequently made stronger. Nevertheless, too many people in the United States and other countries do not have clean drinking water. We must solve this problem in the twenty-first century if we hope to survive.

In the 1900s, people thought that nuclear energy was the answer to the world's decreasing sources of fossil fuel, which is fuel that is formed from natural remains, such as from plants and animals. Unfortunately, the use of nuclear energy created a bigger problem: what to do with the waste that comes from making it. This waste can have dangerous effects on humans and other life forms for thousands of years. The solution was to store it underground in areas that are not likely to have earthquakes, but no one knows for sure if the waste will remain contained. An even bigger problem for the land is the millions of tons of garbage that people create every year. There are landfills and garbage dumps, but the amount of garbage is still increasing, and the people of the United States and other developed nations (those who create the vast majority of the garbage in the world) must solve this problem in the next century. Many countries have begun strong recycling efforts, but it is only the beginning. The goal should be to recycle 100 percent of our garbage.

toxic: poisonous	**contaminated**: made dirty	**contained**: in one closed space
grave: very serious	**subsequently**: to follow closey	

Peer Help Worksheet

Check off each step as you complete it.

1. Which of your partner's concluding paragraphs is the most effective, in your opinion? Why?

2. Look at your partner's first paragraph.
   a. Which of the three ways to conclude does it use?
      (Check all that apply.)
      Summary (Are all the points of the body paragraphs included?) . . . . ❑
      Restatement of the thesis statement
      (Circle the synonyms used.) . . . . ❑
      Final comment . . . . ❑
   b. Is there any new information? If so, underline it.
      Suggest how it might be eliminated. . . . . ❑

3. Look at your partner's second paragraph.
   a. Which of the three ways to conclude does it use?
      (Check all that apply.)
      Summary (Are all the points of the body paragraphs included?) . . . . ❑
      Restatement of the thesis statement
      (Circle the synonyms used.) . . . . ❑
      Final comment . . . . ❑
   b. Is there any new information? If so, underline it.
      Suggest how it might be eliminated. . . . . ❑

4. Reread the two paragraphs and note all the commas.
   a. Are they used correctly? Circle any that you think might
      be incorrect. . . . . ❑
   b. Are there any places that you think need a comma?
      Put a circle with a *C* inside it in places that you think
      need a comma. . . . . ❑

CHAPTER 10 Body Paragraphs

▶ Population and the Environment

Has your home country's population increased, decreased, or basically stayed the same over the past fifty years? If it has changed, what was the approximate population in 1950 and what is it today? If it has stayed the same, are there other changes in the population in your country?

Share your answers to these questions with your classmates. If you have classmates from other countries, discuss how population statistics vary among countries.

1. What is your home country? _____

2. What was that country's population in 1950 (approximately)? _____

3. What is that country's population now (approximately)? _____

4. Have the demographics in your country changed (for example, more or fewer older people, more or fewer poor people, etc.)? _____
   _____

5. How has the changing population affected the environment? _____
   _____

Concrete Support

One of the main problems in essay writing is finding good ideas to support your thesis statement. Without sufficient support, an essay becomes **vague**, or too general. Because a thesis statement is always an opinion, the writer has to convince the reader with concrete facts, examples, and statistics.

Read the essay "Six Billion and Counting" and notice that the body paragraphs lack specific detail. This essay is vague because the writer hasn't given enough support for the reader to be convinced.

Six Billion and Counting

On Tuesday, October 12, 1999, a baby named Adnan was born in Sarajevo, Bosnia-Herzegovina. Adnan was just one of 370,000 babies born that Tuesday, but his birth was a milestone for the world; he was named the world's six-billionth human being. From a world of 1 billion in 1804 and 3 billion in 1960, we reached

6 billion less than forty years later. This very rapid population growth is having serious effects on our food supply, our environment, and our species diversity.

Our growing population is affecting both the total amount of food we have and the distribution of the food to those who need it. Because of improvements in agriculture, we are still increasing the amount of food the world produces, but the rate of increase is slowing down. While people in developing countries often eat too little, people in the Western world eat far too many calories. Getting high-quality food to all those who are in need is a serious concern in a more and more crowded world.

Our skyrocketing population is also leading to serious problems in the quality of the environment. Our waste products are polluting our air, water, and soil. Developed countries are creating many more waste products than developing countries as well as using more of the world's energy. In short, the pressure of our expanding population on our resources is of great concern.

The third effect of our growing population is the crowding out of animal and plant species. In order to make room to build new houses, we are rapidly destroying our forests with all their plant and animal life. As a result, more and more species become extinct every year. When people move into the cleared forest areas, the wild animals that don't get killed have no place to live. Unless we control our population explosion, we will have a world with fewer and fewer species of plants and animals.

The twentieth century saw a population boom never before experienced on our small planet. The impact of this population explosion on our food supply, our environment, and our diversity is beginning to be felt, and many experts believe it will get worse before it gets better. The 1 billion teenagers in the world today will be the people to decide whether to have only the 2.1 children per couple that the world needs to stabilize its population and save our quality of life.

species diversity: the number of different plants and animals that exist	**skyrocketing**: increasing rapidly	**a boom**: a rapid increase
	to crowd out: to have no room for	**an impact**: an effect
a rate: the speed at which something increases or decreases	**extinct**: no longer existing	**to stabilize**: to keep the same; to stop changing

This isn't a bad essay, but it is very general. It needs a few additional facts and examples to make it into a stronger essay. In addition to facts, statistics, and examples, you may want to use examples from your personal life to add support to a thesis statement and make an essay more convincing.

▶ *Practice 1*   Rewriting an Essay

Work with a group of your classmates to rewrite the essay "Six Billion and Counting." Each body paragraph needs more specific support. Look through the facts, statistics, and examples provided on pages 95–97 and choose those that you feel will support the thesis statement and make the essay more specific. There is more information here than

you will want to use, so select carefully. You may also want to use some information that you generate from responding to the personal questions that follow. Rewrite the sentences in the original essay to improve them if necessary.*

Body Paragraph 1: Food Supply and Distribution

<u>Facts and Examples</u>

- In developing countries: 20 percent of the population does not have enough quality food (World Health Organization)
- In the United States: people need
    - 30 percent fewer calories from fats
    - 45 percent fewer calories from refined sugars
    - 70 percent *more* calories from complex carbohydrates (Committee on Nutrition and Human Needs in the U.S. Senate)

<u>Statistics</u>

Table 1:   Food Production Increase over Two Decades

Type of Country	1977–1987		1987–1997	
	Total Increase	Per Person Increase	Total Increase	Per Person Increase
Developed countries	9%	1%	8%	1.7%
Developing countries	41%	12%	33%	7%

<u>Personal Information</u>

1. What kind of food does your country produce?
2. Does it produce enough for the population?

Body Paragraph 2: The Environment

<u>Facts and Examples</u>

- Solid pollution
    - 400 million metric tons of hazardous wastes worldwide every year
- Nuclear pollution: Chernobyl nuclear power plant accident in 1986
    - Serious radioactive pollution to a large part of Europe
    - Approximately 135,000 people evacuated
    - World Health Organization (1995) said the "explosive increase" in childhood cancer in the Ukraine and in Russia directly related to the accident

---

* The information presented here is widely available general knowledge, so it is not necessary to document the sources; in other words, you don't have to say where the information came from. However, when you get information from outside sources that is specific to the source, you usually have to document your research in your paper. Look at any writer's handbook for information on how to document your research.

- Global warming
  - Estimated to cause an increase in the sea level of 3 feet during this century due to population pressure
  - May displace up to 72 million people in China and 71 million people in Bangladesh
- Overuse of water
  - In India, water level in the ground is falling by 1 to 3 meters per year
  - India's population expanding at the rate of 18 million people annually

Statistics

Table 2: Annual per Person Household Waste in Selected Countries

Country	Tons of Domestic Waste	Kilograms per Person
United States	200,000,000	875
Australia	10,000,000	680
Canada	12,600,000	525
Norway	1,700,000	415
Japan	40,225,000	288
Spain	8,028,000	214

Table 3: Annual World Commercial Energy Consumption

Region	Millions of Metric Tons of Oil	Percent of Total World Consumption
United States	1,626	24.1%
Europe	1,537	22.7%
Commonwealth of Independent States (formerly the USSR)	1,307	19.3%
Africa, Saudi Arabia, Iraq, Iran, India, Australia	898	13.3%
China	561	8.3%
South America and Latin America	330	4.9%
Japan	319	4.7%
Canada	180	2.7%

Personal Information

1. What are the major environmental problems facing your country?
2. What is your government doing to help solve these problems?

Body Paragraph 3: Species Extinction

Facts and Examples

- Rain forests
    - About 100,000 square kilometers (40,000 square miles) destroyed every year.
    - < 2% of the Atlantic coastal rain forest of Brazil remains today
- Species extinction
    - In 1900, an estimated 50,000 to 80,000 tigers in India alone
    - In 1998, fewer than 5,000 tigers worldwide

Statistics

Table 4: Increase in Species Extinction

Year	Number of Species Becoming Extinct
1700	1
1800	1
1900	1
1950	5
1970	200
1990	5,000
2000	50,000

Personal Information

1. Do you feel that species diversity is important? Why or why not?
2. What species are endangered in your country?

Topic Sentences and Concluding Sentences in Body Paragraphs

In Part I of this book, you learned that individual paragraphs start with a topic sentence and end with a concluding sentence. This is usually true for stand-alone paragraphs, but it is not always true for body paragraphs in an essay.

Sometimes you may not need a topic sentence for each body paragraph. This can happen when the thesis statement for the essay has a predictor and clearly shows what the topic for each paragraph will be.

Example

There are three actions anyone can take to help decrease our garbage problem: reduce the amount you throw away, reuse items that are still good, and recycle things that can be recycled.

The thesis statement in the example on page 97 indicates by its predictor that there will be three body paragraphs in this essay and that they will deal with reducing, reusing, and recycling. Those three body paragraphs will come in the order mentioned in the thesis statement. It is important to maintain the unity of each body paragraph when you are not using a topic sentence.

If it is not a topic sentence, the first sentence of a body paragraph may function as a connection, or **bridge**, between one paragraph and another. If the first sentence is a bridge, then the second sentence may or may not be a topic sentence. In addition, concluding sentences in body paragraphs are not always required. The last sentence of a body paragraph may also function as a bridge to the following paragraph.

▶ *Practice 2*   Analyzing an Essay

Read the following essay. First, underline the thesis statement. Then, as you read, consider these questions.

1. What is the function of the first sentence in each body paragraph? Is it a topic sentence? Is it a bridge?

2. What is the purpose of the last sentence in each body paragraph? Is it a topic sentence? Is it a bridge?

Greenpeace: Defender of the Environment

The Greenpeace Foundation is an organization of ordinary people and scientists from around the world who are active in efforts to expose and find solutions for global environmental problems. The organization was started in the early 1970s in an effort to defend human, animal, and plant life. Greenpeace has had steady, if small, successes in decreasing whale hunting, saving old forests, and cutting down on the toxic pollution of our air and water.

Greenpeace works hard to protect the quality of our oceans and their populations of fish, mammals, and vegetation. The year 2000 marked the twenty-fifth anniversary of the organization's fight to keep many whale populations from becoming extinct. Since 1975, when a Greenpeace ship confronted a Soviet whaling ship off the coast of California, Greenpeace activists have regularly positioned themselves between the whale and the hunting boat to protect the whale. These small protests have proven successful in that the whale population is again slowly increasing. This very personal type of protest has been successful for Greenpeace elsewhere as well.

Ancient forests, according to Greenpeace, are forest areas that are relatively undisturbed by human activity. By 1999, more than 80 percent of the world's original ancient forests had been destroyed. An example of such an ancient forest is the Great Bear Rain Forest, which covers western Canada. This forest was mainly damaged by a logging method called clear-cutting, which means that every single tree in a large area is cut down at the same time.

Clear-cutting in the Great Bear Rain Forest has caused the population of grizzly bears to almost disappear, and it has reduced the populations of salmon in the rivers by two-thirds. Greenpeace members put themselves between the trees and the tree cutters. They experienced a victory on August 26, 1999, when the U.S. company Home Depot, a major buyer of wood from the Great Bear Rain Forest, announced that it would stop selling wood products from rain forests. Although this was only a small step in the process of protecting the forests we have left, it was still a significant event.

What About You?

What is the name of an environmental protection organization in your neighborhood or country? What is its purpose?

However, the major threat to vegetation, animals, and people is now neither hunting nor cutting. It is the extremely toxic chemicals that our industrial society releases into both air and water. Greenpeace has helped local people in affected areas to protest against companies that produce such pollution. One small victory happened in Louisiana in the late 1990s. For three years, the Japanese plastics company Shintech had tried to establish PVC factories next to schools and homes in the small town of Convent, Louisiana. PVC is a common type of plastic used in everything from children's toys to kitchen containers. PVC itself is safe, but the manufacturing of it gives off a waste product called dioxin, which is an extremely toxic chemical. With the help of Greenpeace, the citizens of Convent won their battle in September of 1998, when Shintech withdrew its plans to build the factories.

In conclusion, each victory gives us hope, but they are indeed small when contrasted with the problems we face. Even so, Greenpeace activists fight on, and their efforts in preventing whale hunting, protecting ancient forests, and limiting the use of dangerous chemicals are showing some positive effects. Because of Greenpeace, the world will be a little safer for our children and our children's children.

to confront: to argue with; to behave in a threatening way toward someone or something

ancient: very old

logging: cutting down trees to use for lumber, paper, and other products

significant: important

toxic: poisonous

PVC: an abbreviation for *polyvinyl chloride*

victory: the success achieved by winning

Mechanics

Punctuation Errors

In Parts I and II of this book, you learned about how to use commas and semicolons, and how to correct the common errors of fragments, comma splices, and run-on sentences. Practice 3 on the next page reviews common punctuation problems.

▶ *Practice 3* Analyzing Punctuation Errors

Find and correct the punctuation problems in the paragraph below. You will need to:

- add eight commas*
- delete two commas
- correct one fragment
- correct one comma splice with a semicolon
- correct one run-on sentence

* *Note*: The comma preceding the last item in a list is optional.

Watching Pets

There are three main kinds of animals that people keep in cages or glass tanks so that they can watch them: birds reptiles and rodents. Because they are colorful and graceful to look at. Birds are very popular. In my country, some people have only one big bird in a cage but others have several small ones fluttering and chirping around in a single cage. I would never consider having a reptile, such as a snake, in my house, however a friend of mine has a boa constrictor in a cage, and swears that it is a lovely pet, since it doesn't bark doesn't eat much and never needs to be taken out for a walk. Finally, rodents are another kind of animal that can be kept in a cage. Rodents are small animals like guinea pigs gerbils and hamsters they are especially popular with children. If they are treated properly they can live quite a long time. In short these animals have a fascination for people who mostly like to watch their pets.

▶ *Writing To Communicate*

Choose one of these essay topics as this chapter's writing assignment.

1. The most serious environmental problem facing my country today
2. How every one of us can help clean up the environment
3. A comparison of the quality of the environment in two cities you know
4. How attitudes toward the environment have changed in your country since your parents were young
5. How the population is changing in your country and the effect this has on everyone's lifestyle

Be sure to follow these steps when writing your essay.

- Assess the assignment—what have you been asked to do?
- Generate ideas for the topic.

- Write an essay plan in your favorite form.

- Think seriously about your thesis statement. Write it on a separate piece of paper first.

- Think of your introduction. How do you want to "hook" your reader?

- Organize your support of the thesis statement. What are your main points?

- Add interesting and persuasive support. You should use support that you already know. No research is required.

- Use a simple conclusion to summarize the points in your body paragraphs or paraphrase your thesis statement. You may want to add a final comment.

Peer Help Worksheet

Check off each step as you complete it.

1 What did you find most interesting about this essay?

2 The type of support used in this essay is: (Check all that apply.)

Facts . . . . ❑

Examples . . . . ❑

Statistics . . . . ❑

Personal information . . . . ❑

3 Organization

a. Does the essay have a thesis statement with a

   Topic? If it does, underline it. . . . . ❑

   Controlling idea? If it does, circle it. . . . . ❑

b. How many body paragraphs does this essay

   have? _____ . . . . ❑

c. Does each have a topic sentence? If yes, underline

   the topic sentence. . . . . ❑

   If not, is it clear from the thesis statement what the topic

   of this paragraph is? . . . . ❑

d. What is the function of the last sentence in each body

   paragraph? Is it a true concluding sentence, or is it

   a bridge to the next paragraph? . . . . ❑

4 Editing

a. Is this essay written with correct paragraph format? . . . . ❑

b. Is the separation between paragraphs clear? . . . . ❑

PART III RHETORICAL PATTERNS

RELATIONSHIPS

CHAPTER 11 Process

▶

Love

The word *relationship* is defined as "the quality or state of being connected; the way in which people or groups behave toward each other; or a situation in which two people have romantic feelings for each other." Do you remember how it feels when you are first in love? It's not surprising that we say "to fall in love" because it feels like falling. When you think of loving and being loved, do you associate any special things with those feelings? Perhaps you think about eating a romantic meal, wearing special clothes, or listening to a certain type of music. With your classmates, discuss your favorite things about being in love.

Prewriting

In this chapter, you will practice writing essays that describe a **process**. In this type of essay, you tell the reader how to do something or you report on something that has happened, such as an experiment. You describe step by step what someone should do or what you have done to achieve a certain result. To write this type of essay well, it is important to make sure that all the steps are covered and that they are presented in chronological order.

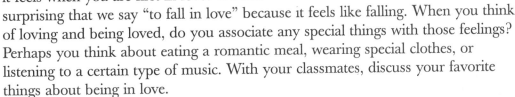
▶ *Practice 1* **The Food of Love**

The American saying "The way to a man's heart is through his stomach" shows how important food can be in romance. Cultures around the world traditionally consider different types of food to be romantic. What would you serve for a romantic dinner? Ask other students in the class to describe any foods that are unfamiliar to you. When you are finished, discuss the results with your classmates.

    1. As an appetizer, I would serve

        a. oysters

        b. raw vegetables

        c. salted nuts

        d. other: _____

    2. As the first course, I would serve

        a. hot and sour soup

        b. shrimp cocktail

        c. tomato salad

        d. other: _____

3. To drink with dinner, I would serve

    a. wine

    b. green tea

    c. champagne

    d. other: _____

4. As the main course, I would serve

    a. steak

    b. lasagna

    c. Peking duck

    d. other: _____

5. As dessert, I would serve

    a. ice cream

    b. fresh fruit

    c. tiramisu

    d. other: _____

Graphic Organizers

Since an essay that describes a process is essentially a "how to" essay, it is always arranged chronologically. The number of paragraphs depends on how you organize your information. Some essays are very simple and have only three paragraphs: an introduction, a long body paragraph, and a conclusion. In other essays, you can have two, three, or even more body paragraphs. For example:

Process Essay Organizer 1: How to Cook a Superior Steak

Introductory paragraph
Thesis statement: Cooking an excellent steak is easy if you follow these five steps.

Long body paragraph
All the steps in the correct chronological order.

Concluding paragraph
Essay conclusion

Process Essay Organizer 2: How to Dance the Waltz

Introductory paragraph
Thesis statement: If I can learn to waltz, so can you—if you remember a few simple steps.

Body paragraph 1
The basic components of the waltz

Body paragraph 2
The waltz steps

Concluding paragraph
Essay conclusion

Process Essay Organizer 3: How to Make Taffy

Introductory paragraph
Thesis statement: Making taffy is very easy if you follow these steps.

Body paragraph 1
Ingredients and equipment

Body paragraph 2
Mixing the candy

Body paragraph 3
What to do after you have cooked the candy

Concluding paragraph
Essay conclusion

Freewriting

 Practice 2 How to . . .

What do you know how to do well? It could be cooking something, repairing something, putting something together, making something, or playing a sport. In this practice, you are going to give instructions to someone about how to do something that the person does not do well. For five minutes, think about the materials or ingredients you need and all the steps involved. Then start writing. Don't stop for ten minutes! You may want to refer back to this assignment when you are writing your process essay later in this chapter.

Model Essays

Read the model process essays that follow.

Model Essay 1 ────────────────────────────

How to Cook a Superior Steak

My girlfriend Alicia loves meat. While other women choose raw vegetables and nonfat yogurt, she orders a huge steak every time we go out. Because these restaurant meals were getting pretty expensive, I decided to learn to cook her favorite food at home. Cooking an excellent steak is easy if you follow these five steps.

First, you should do your shopping carefully. A cooked steak is only as good as the cut of meat you select. Choose the best cut you can afford. Second, when you get the steak home, measure the thickness. The third step is to heat the grill so that it is extremely hot. Then, put the steak on the very hot grill and immediately turn it over to brown it on both sides. Since Alicia likes her steak very pink in the center, I have learned to cook her steak no more than ten minutes per inch of thickness. This locks in the juices and makes it tender. Finally, never answer the telephone while cooking steak because it can easily get overcooked. A rare steak is best, and Alicia won't have it any other way.

Since Alicia doesn't cook, she doesn't know how easy this meal is. She thinks I am a great chef! If you follow these directions, you can make someone happy, too. Enjoy eating your delicious steak!

What About You?

Do you like to eat meat? If so, is this how you cook it? If not, what is your favorite food to cook?

Model Essay 2 ────────────────────────────

How to Dance the Waltz

I'll never forget the agony of my first waltz. I was twelve years old, and it occurred at my sister's wedding. My mother forced me to ask my bossy cousin Mary to dance. Naturally, both of us tried to lead. This proved to be quite unsuccessful as well as embarrassing. Therefore, I signed up for dancing school the next day. If I can learn to waltz, so can you—if you remember a few simple steps.

The most important thing I learned in dancing school was to move slowly. There is no need to hurry a waltz. Second, as my cousin needed to learn, the man always leads in the waltz. Finally, if you are a beginner, you should count off the steps in your head. Say to yourself "One, two, three; one, two, three" over and over. Now that you have mastered these three basics, you can go on to the actual movement of the feet.

The waltz pattern is basically a square. If you are a woman, start by moving your right foot one step backward. If you are a man, start by moving your left foot forward. Then make one step sideways to the woman's left. Then both partners move their feet together. Next, if you are a woman, you move your left foot forward while the man moves his right foot backward. Finally, you both make one step sideways to the man's left, and you'll find that you're back where you started! Do it again and move around a little on the dance floor.

Of course this is only the basic waltz. There are lots of variations, but the key to the waltz is still the "one, two, three" beat of the music. My dancing school lessons definitely paid off when I saw my cousin again a month ago at another wedding and asked her to dance. She was pleasantly surprised. I can dance!

What About You?

Do you like traditional dances? Many people don't, but sometimes they are "a must" at weddings and festivals. Describe the steps of a traditional dance in your culture.

bossy: always telling other people what to do

to lead: when dancing, to guide your partner

Model Essay 3

How to Make Taffy

Americans are well known for their love for sweet things. They love chocolate, ice cream, cakes, and cookies. In fact, they love anything sweet. A traditional American favorite candy is taffy. Making taffy is very easy if you follow these steps.

First, you need to assemble the ingredients and the equipment. You'll need sugar, corn syrup, cornstarch, butter, salt, and vanilla. You will also need a 2-quart saucepan and a square 8 x 8 inch cakepan. In addition, you will need a candy thermometer. (This is a special thermometer that you can put into boiling liquid to measure the temperature.) You'll need scissors and some plastic wrap. Once you have these items, you can start cooking your taffy.

Second, butter the cakepan and set it aside. Mix 1 cup of sugar, 3/4 cup of corn syrup, 2/3 cup of water, 1 tablespoon of cornstarch, 2 tablespoons of butter, and 1 teaspoon of salt in the saucepan. Heat the mixture over medium heat, stirring constantly until it boils. Then, cook it without stirring until the candy thermometer reads 256°F. At this point, remove the pan from the heat, and stir in 2 teaspoons of vanilla. Pour the candy mixture into the cakepan immediately.

After you have cooked this mixture, you need to let it cool for about 15–20 minutes. When it is just cool enough to handle, pull the taffy hard with both hands until it becomes shiny, light in color, and stiff. If it gets sticky, butter your hands a little. Pull it into long strips of about a half inch wide. Cut the strips into pieces with scissors. When you have pulled it like this, wrap each piece in plastic wrap. This is necessary for the candy to hold its shape. When it is completely hard, the final step is easy: Eat a piece and enjoy it.

As you can see, taffy is a kind of candy that is quite simple to make. It is certainly very sweet and only for sugar lovers. Moreover, having a taffy-pull party with your friends can be every bit as much fun as eating it.

Paragraphs in the Process Essay

▶ *Practice 3* Review of Cohesion and Introductory Paragraphs

Remember that sentences in a paragraph must have cohesion; that is, they have to be connected to each other. As you learned in Chapter 4, there are five cohesive devices: linking words, personal pronouns, the definite article, demonstrative pronouns, and synonyms. Read the introductory paragraph from Model Essay 2 on page 106 again, sentence by sentence. Identify the cohesive devices.

Sentence	Cohesive Device
1. I'll never forget the agony of my first waltz.	*Use of personal pronoun "my."*
2. I was twelve years old, and it occurred at my sister's wedding.	
3. My mother forced me to ask my bossy cousin Mary to dance.	
4. Naturally, both of us tried to lead.	
5. This proved to be quite unsuccessful as well as embarrassing.	
6. Therefore, I signed up for dancing school the next day.	
7. If I with can learn to waltz, so can you—if you remember a few simple steps.	

Chronological Linking Words

Linking words make a piece of writing hold together as a text. They help connect sentences. There are several different types of linking words: transitions, conjunctions, and prepositions. Their grammatical functions are:

• Transitions	connect two independent clauses
• Conjunctions	
Subordinate conjunctions	introduce adverb clauses
Coordinate conjunctions	connect two independent clauses
• Prepositions	precede nouns or noun phrases

The following chart lists some common linking words used in essays that describe a process.

Transitions	Conjunctions		Prepositions
	Subordinate	Coordinate	
first second at first next after that later on finally at this point	after before while when since	and	after before since in addition to prior to

▶ *Practice 4* **Adding Linking Words**

Read the ten steps below describing the process "How to Make Scrambled Eggs." Then, write the sentences below and on page 110 using the linking words given in parentheses. Note that the steps are in the imperative. You will need to change the imperative verbs into present tense verbs when you use conjunctions as linking words.

1. Break 3 eggs in a bowl.

2. Mix them using a wire whisk.

3. Pour in 1 tablespoon of water for each egg.

4. Add a pinch of salt.

5. Heat a frying pan.

6. Melt 1 tablespoon of butter in the pan.

7. Pour in the egg mixture.

8. Stir the eggs by scraping the pan with a spatula.

9. Stop scraping when the eggs are golden yellow.

10. Don't overcook the eggs. Cooking eggs too long makes them rubbery.

Sentence 1 *(first)*

_____

Sentence 2 *(next)*

_____

Sentences 3 and 4 *(after)* [*Note:* Change the imperative verb.]

_____

Sentence 5 *(at this point)*

_____

Sentences 6 and 7 *(after)* [*Note*: Pay attention to the verb tenses.]

_____

Sentences 8 and 9 *(until)*

_____

Sentence 10 *(finally)*

_____

▶ *Practice 5*   Using Commas in a Process Paragraph

This paragraph needs seven more commas. Insert commas in the correct places.

Learning to Love Again

When my best friend died in a horrible car accident I thought my heart would be broken forever. It felt like there had been an earthquake and that all my happiness had been crushed beneath a mountain of stones. The way back to life and love was long but I took small steps of improvement along the way. First my mother taught me to appreciate the little things of everyday life, such as the taste of icy cold milk or the smell of my dog's newly washed fur. After a few months I was able to smile at my little sister when she tried so hard to please me. Every week, my grandfather drove me to the cemetery where my friend's grave was and I finally realized how kind he was to me. Much later, I actually went to eat pizza with my classmates and even enjoyed myself. That was when I began to understand that my friend wouldn't have wanted me to fall apart in my unhappiness; he would have wanted me to continue in life. Therefore when I met someone I really liked I agreed to go out with him. It took a whole year, but I have learned to love again.

a cemetery: a large piece of land where dead people are buried   **a grave**: a place where a dead body is buried

▶ *Writing To Communicate*

Now, it's your turn to write a process essay. Choose one of these three topics. If none of them appeal to you, ask your teacher if you can choose a topic from "Other Essays" on pages 112–113. Write an essay about one page long, or about 300 words, double-spaced. If you need help getting started, review the steps of "The Writing Process" at the bottom of this page.

1. Creating a Romantic Evening for Two

   Think about the ingredients (such as soft music, candles, great food), the preparation (such as getting a baby-sitter and going to the hairdresser), and the activities (such as going to the theater or taking a slow walk in the park hand in hand).

2. How to Be Happy Without Romantic Love

   Love happens when we least expect it, but what about all the times in between? Think about the "prescription" you would give for being happy without being in love. [*Note*: A prescription is what a doctor writes out for you to get medicine that helps you feel better and stay healthy.]

3. Reaching Out to Someone You Can't Stand

   It's easy to love people whose behavior and opinions are similar to ours. Yet we all know there are many people in the world that we simply don't like. What are the steps you need to take to begin a friendship with someone you dislike?

The Writing Process

- First, review the three types of graphic organizers on pages 104–105 and decide which one you want to use.

- Next, write an outline of your essay. What will your thesis statement be?

- Think about your introduction. You want to grab the reader's attention. Perhaps you can use a surprising fact or statistic, or perhaps you can think of a funny anecdote to begin your essay.

- Now, write the first draft of your essay, paying particular attention to linking words and verb tenses.

- Finally, check your spelling, comma use, and layout. Make sure you have centered your essay title and that you have appropriate margins on both sides of the paper. The margins should be at least 1 inch on the left and on the right. It is also customary to leave 1 to 2 inches at the top of the page and 1 inch at the bottom.

Peer Help Worksheet

Check off each step as you complete it.

1 What did you like most about this essay?

2 Organization

    a. Does the essay have a thesis statement with a

        Topic? If it does, underline it. . . . . ❑

        Controlling idea? If it does, circle it. . . . . ❑

    b. Does the essay have an introductory paragraph? What kind?

        Personal anecdote . . . . ❑

        Third-person anecdote . . . . ❑

        Interesting facts or statistics . . . . ❑

        Historical information . . . . ❑

        General to specific . . . . ❑

    c. How many steps are listed in the process? _____

        Are they in the correct order? . . . . ❑

    d. Does the concluding paragraph

        (Check all that apply.)

        Restate the thesis? . . . . ❑

        Summarize the steps? . . . . ❑

        Give a final comment? . . . . ❑

3 Editing

    a. Does the essay have problems with punctuation, such as

        fragments, comma splices, and run-on sentences? . . . . ❑

    b. Is the grammar used with chronological linking words

        correct? . . . . ❑

Other Essays

Process writing can be long and complicated, or it can be short and simple. It can be a whole book (e.g., Dale Carnegie's *How to Win Friends and Influence People*), a medium-length article in a magazine ("How to Lose 10 Pounds in 10 Days" or "How to Succeed in Business"), or just a list of steps to program your VCR. Here are some other topics that lend themselves to a process organizational pattern. Choose one and write an essay about it.

1. Sports and Games

All over the world, people play games in their free time. These games can range from simple children's games, like jumping rope, to such complex adult games as chess and tennis. Think of a fairly simple sport or game that you know well and write an essay describing how to play it. Consider the following:

- What equipment do you need?

- What are the main rules of the game?

- How do you play the game to win?

2. Preparing for and Surviving Disasters

Natural disasters can happen anytime and anywhere. How can you be well prepared for such a disaster? What could you do before, during, and after it to increase your chances of survival? Choose from these natural disasters: earthquakes, mudslides, avalanches, hailstorms, tornadoes, hurricanes, floods, and snowstorms. Write an essay explaining how you can prepare for and survive this disaster. Consider the following:

- How can you best prepare for a disaster?

- What supplies would you need to survive until help comes? (food, water, heat source, clothes, medical supplies, etc.)

- How can you make your home safe in a disaster?

- What kind of plan should you make to contact family or friends?

- What should you do and not do during the disaster?

- What are the first things to do to recover from the disaster?

3. Tongue-in-Cheek

Try to write a funny essay in which you describe the opposite of what people usually want. Consider the following:

- How to fail a test

- How to gain 50 pounds

- How to be a boring person

- How to ditch your boyfriend or girlfriend

- How to make a lot of enemies

CHAPTER 12 Classification

▶

Family and Work

What makes one family different from another? It could be who makes up the family or where the family lives. It might be a trait, such as hair color, interests or skills, or personality types. It may even be the unique relationships that family members have with each other. A second theme of this chapter is the relationships we have at work and in our personal lives. In your experience, are friendships at work different from friendships outside of work? Discuss your thoughts about family and work with your classmates.

Prewriting

The verb *classify* means, "to divide objects, people, or ideas into groups or categories." It is something we all do every day. You might organize movies into those you like and those you don't like; you might divide people you know into those who are outgoing and those who are quiet; and you might classify music into classical, rock and roll, country, rap, and so on.

It is important to note that you always classify according to a principle even though you may not be aware of it. For example, consider the topic of *boats*. If you want to write an essay classifying boats, you have to state the **subject** you are describing (boats), the **classification principle** (for example, how they move), and the **categories** (in this case: sailboats, powerboats, rowboats).

▶ *Practice 1* **Classification Principles**

Look at the chart on page 115, which lists *subject*, *classification principle*, *number of categories*, and *category names*. With a partner, add another classification principle, number of categories, and category names for each of the three subjects.

Subject	Classification Principle	Number of Categories	Category Names
Buildings	use	six	office, residential, factory, school, arts, storage
Buildings			
Paintings	material	two	water based, oil based
Paintings			
Pets	number of legs	three	four legs, two legs, no legs
Pets			

▶ *Practice 2* Classifying People

With a partner, add two more classification principles as well as the numbers and names of the categories.

Subject	Classification Principle	Number of Categories	Category Names
People	age	five	child, teenager, young adult, middle-aged adult, senior citizen
People			
People			

▶ *Practice 3* Determining the Classification Principle

The classification principle is understood, but not stated, in these five thesis statements. Circle the classification principle. Then, compare your answers with a classmate's answers.

1. There are two types of high schools in the United States: public and private.

    a. quality of instruction

    b. qualification of the teachers

    c. who pays for the schools

2. Deep-sea fishing, shore fishing, and river fishing are the kinds of fishing most people enjoy.

   a. size of fish you catch

   b. where you do the fishing

   c. how much you like the activity

3. Modern countries are either democracies or dictatorships.

   a. how the leader got into power

   b. whether the country is ruled by royalty or a president

   c. how safe the people are

4. The four major food groups are: grains and nuts, fruits and vegetables, dairy products, and animal products.

   a. the freshness of the food

   b. the origin of the food

   c. the healthfulness of the food

▶ *Practice 4* **Writing Classification Thesis Statements**

Write the categories for classifying each of the following three groups by using the principle given. One of the categories in each has been done as an example. Then, write a thesis statement for each group. [*Note*: Under "Categories" you may need more or fewer lines than the four that are given.]

Example

Subject: Books

Principle: Truth value

Categories: ____fiction____   ____nonfiction____

Thesis statement: _Books can be divided into fiction and nonfiction based on_

                   their truth value.

1. Subject: Vehicles

   Principle: Number of wheels

   Categories: ____two____   _____

                   _____   _____

   Thesis statement: _____

                     _____

2. Subject: Feeling safe

   Principle: Providers

   Categories: _police department_   _____

                   _____ _____

   Thesis statement: _____

                     _____

3. Subject: Colleges

   Principle: Admission criteria

   Categories: _high school grades_   _____

                   _____ _____

   Thesis statement: _____

                     _____

Graphic Organizers

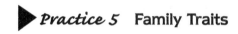 **Practice 5 Family Traits**

Look at this sample of a family tree.

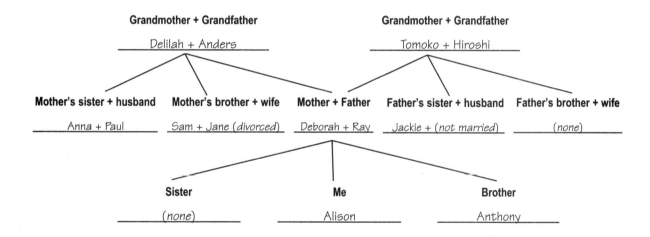

Complete your own family tree in the diagram on the next page. Write your name under the word *Me*. Then, write in the names of your relatives. You may need to add a few people; for example, you may have more than one brother or sister, and your parents may have many brothers and sisters as well. You can begin with the diagram here, but you'll probably need a separate sheet of paper.

My Family Tree

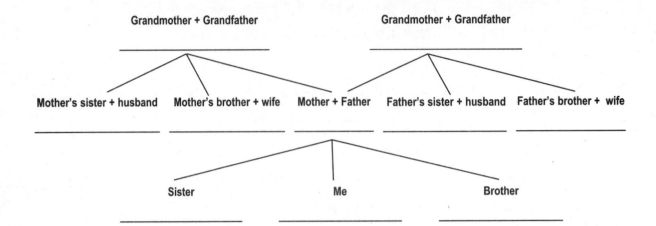

Now, think of and make notes about your family's traits. Do you share any characteristics with your relatives? For example, do you have the same hair as your mother's mother? (That's your *maternal grandmother*, or *Delilah*, in the example on page 117.) Do you have your father's personality? How about you and your brother or sister? Does your brother or sister share any special interests with you? List your family characteristics (or *traits*) below.

Example

Appearance	(*shared with*)	Interests	(*shared with*)	Skills	(*shared with*)
straight,	mother	sports	brother	fishing	grandfather
black hair					

Appearance	(*shared with*)	Interests	(*shared with*)	Skills	(*shared with*)

 Practice 6   **Writing a Paragraph That Classifies**

Write a paragraph in which you classify your family traits into the categories of appearance, interests, and skills. Give examples of family members with whom you share the traits you describe.

Freewriting

 Practice 7   **Fifteen-Minute Freewriting**

Take out a notepad or notebook and get ready to write. The topic is *My Friends: A Classification*. Don't worry about grammar or punctuation at this point—the idea is just to

get sentences down on paper. Try to write continuously for fifteen minutes without stopping to take your pen off the paper. When you are finished, put your freewriting away. You may want to refer back to this assignment when you are writing your classification essay later in the chapter.

Model Essays

Read the model classification essays that follow.

Model Essay 1 ──────────────────────────────

No Man Is an Island
"No man is an island, entire of itself."
—John Donne, 1572–1631

Sometimes, I wish that I were adopted and that I didn't know who my parents were. Then, no one could say, "Your cousin Thomas gets all A's in school, so why can't you?" or "That hair of yours is just like your grandmother's; there's nothing you can do about it." The truth is that I'm not adopted, and even though I try to fight against it, I see family traits in myself all the time. The three main personality types in my family are athletic, studious, and materialistic.

My father and his brother (my uncle Jonas) are athletic. They're both tall and thin even though they love to eat. My father gets up at 5 A.M. every Sunday to drive two hours to a golf course. On weekdays, he parks his car three miles away from his office just so he can walk to work in heavy city traffic swinging his briefcase and whistling. My uncle Jonas is a terror on the basketball court. Even when he's playing with his seven-year old son, he plays to win. I know that some of that competitiveness has come down to me because even if I don't play sports seriously, I can't stand losing.

The studious types in my family are the ones everybody talks about. My cousin Anna Louise, for example, is a "goody-goody" high school student who wins every school prize there is. I don't like Anna Louise because we have absolutely nothing to talk about. All she knows about life is what she has read in a textbook. My brother is also studious, but he's totally different from Anna Louise. He's great with computers. He can fix anything electronic. Naturally, he gets top honors in all his science and math classes, but he hates history. I remember once he was going to have a test about World War II, and one of the study questions asked whether it was in the 1800s, 1900s, or 2000s. His response was: "Who cares, as long as there isn't a third one." I admire him for that answer although I'm sure his teacher wasn't very happy.

My mother's two sisters and their children are the materialistic ones in our family. I don't know where they got that trait from; it certainly wasn't from my grandparents. My maternal grandparents are sweet and gentle and not the least bit selfish. However, these two aunts have brought their kids up to believe that the only things that are valuable in the world can be counted in money. Every time I'm with these cousins, they talk about how much their new watch cost or how much money they'll make when they go into business like their dads. After two hours of that, I just have to get away.

Still, to be honest, I must say I have a little of all these traits in myself as well. I'm not naturally athletic, but on a tennis court I'll drive myself to a heart attack rather than lose. Although I'm not a straight-A student, I can study when I need to. I do love reading novels, especially science fiction. I like to say that my motivation for wanting to study medicine is to help make the world a better place, but I have to admit that the salary is pretty nice as well. In short, I see a little bit of myself in all my relatives whether I like it or not.

What About You?

Are there any personality characteristics in your family that most members share? Do you think your personality would be different if you had grown up in a different family?

competitiveness: determination to win at something and be more successful than others

studious: spending a lot of time reading and studying

"goody-goody": someone who likes to seem good when others are watching

materialistic: believing that money and possessions are the most important things

---

▶ Practice 8   Questions about "No Man Is an Island"

Answer the following questions.

1. What is the subject that is classified in this essay?

   _____

2. What is the classification principle?

   _____

3. How many categories does the writer divide the subject into: two, three, four, five, or is it unclear? _____

4. What are the names of the categories in this essay?

   _____

Model Essay 2

May I Help You?

The world is rapidly changing from an industrial economy to a service economy. There are fewer and fewer small factories and farms. As a result, a decreasing number of people are employed in manufacturing. How many shoemakers or bakers do you know? You probably don't know any, but you do know the advertising people for the shoemakers and the salespeople for oven manufacturers. In a service economy such as ours, there are service providers and consumers, who receive a service. According to the authority of the provider, there are three basic relationships between service providers and consumers: customer and salesperson, student and teacher, and patient and doctor.

In the retail industry, people often say, "The customer is always right." What they mean is that a salesperson never argues with a customer. If a 350-pound man wants to buy a pink bikini swimsuit, that's his business. The salesperson is there to make the customer feel good about shopping at that particular store so that he'll come back again and again. A salesperson can try to interest the customer in a different style, but he never tells the customer what to do. In the service relationship between the customer and the salesperson, the customer has all the authority.

The relationship between a student and a teacher is different all over the world. It also varies depending on the age of the student. We tend to accept that "the teacher is always right" through the years of obligatory education. However, once people are old enough to make some choices about their education, the relationship changes. If you want to learn tai chi, for example, you will probably look for a teacher that suits your style. Nevertheless, you still believe that your teacher knows much more about the subject than you do, so in this service relationship, the teacher has a medium level of authority.

Certain service providers have such specialized skills and knowledge that we tend to allow them complete authority in making decisions about what's best. The doctor–patient relationship is an example of such a relationship. We expect (rightly or wrongly) that the doctor is so much of an expert that if she says, "You need surgery," we usually don't say, "No, thank you." However, the medical profession is changing as many patients are becoming better educated about their conditions. It is now common practice in many parts of the world to get a second doctor's opinion about how to treat an illness. Even so, in the traditional doctor–patient relationship, it is the doctor who has most of, if not all, the authority.

Most of us will be on both sides in a service relationship at some point in our lives. You may be a customer at noon and a salesperson at 1 P.M. You may be a teacher at age twenty-eight and a student at age fifty-eight. If you become an expert in a certain field, such as engineering, medicine, law, or psychology, you may be a client or patient one day and the service provider the next. However, you will never be both at the same time, and providing great service to your clients will still be based on the fundamental principle of understanding what your customer wants and needs.

| **manufacturing**: the process of making goods in factories | **retail**: the sale of goods in stores to people for their own use | **obligatory**: required; having to be done because of a rule or law |
| | | **fundamental**: basic |

▶ *Practice 9* **Questions about "May I Help You?"**

Answer the following questions.

1. What is the subject that is classified in this essay?

2. What is the classification principle?

_____

3. How many categories does the writer divide the subject into: two, three, four, five, or is it unclear? _____

4. What are the names of the categories in this essay?

_____

Paragraphs in the Classification Essay

How do you turn a simple classification into a full-length essay? The best way is to choose detailed examples and descriptions to convince your reader that your categories are reasonable. For example, let's say that you have divided the group "my friends" into three categories: the *worrywarts* (people who worry all the time about everything), the *bookworms* (people who study all the time), and the *fatalists* (people who feel that life is outside their control). Your thesis statement is that all of your friends fall into one of these three groups. First, you need to define the categories. Next, you need to show your reader exactly what makes the people in one group different from those in the other two. To do this you think: "How does a worrywart act? How does this person feel and behave in certain situations in which the others would feel and behave very differently? How do I feel when I am with a person like this?" The answers to those kinds of questions will lead you to the illustrations you can use to support your thesis statement.

▶ *Practice 10*   **Body Paragraphs in a Classification Essay**

With your classmates, discuss what people do in the following situations. Write notes next to each category.

1. It's 8:00 A.M., and the writing class starts at 8:30 A.M. The bus should have left at 7:45 A.M., but it's late, and your friend won't get to class on time. What would this person do?

   a worrywart: _____

   a bookworm: _____

   a fatalist: _____

2. Your friend was in a car accident. He wasn't hurt badly, but the insurance company says it was his fault, and it won't pay for the damages to his car. What would this person do?

a worrywart: _____

a bookworm: _____

a fatalist: _____

3. The International TOEFL® Test is two weeks from now. Your friend must get a high score to be admitted to her favorite college. What would this person do?

a worrywart: _____

a bookworm: _____

a fatalist: _____

▶ *Practice 11* Outlining an Essay

Complete the following outline of an essay describing your friends as worrywarts, bookworms, and fatalists using the actions and activities you talked about in Practice 10.

Title: My Friends

Introduction: Why I like them all

Thesis: Almost all my friends can be divided into worrywarts, bookworms, or fatalists.

- *Paragraph 1: The worrywarts*

What they do when they're late for something:

_____

_____

What they do when they have money trouble:

_____

_____

What they do when there's an important exam coming up:

_____

_____

- *Paragraph 2: The bookworms*

   What they do when they're late for something:

   _____

   _____

   What they do when they have money trouble:

   _____

   _____

   What they do when there's an important exam coming up:

   _____

   _____

- *Paragraph 3: The fatalists*

   What they do when they're late for something:

   _____

   _____

   What they do when they have money trouble:

   _____

   _____

   What they do when there's an important exam coming up:

   _____

   _____

   Conclusion: Variety is the spice of life.

Linking Words of Example and Consequence

In essays that classify, the use of such linking words as transitions and prepositional phrases of **example** is crucial. In order for your reader to clearly grasp how you are classifying, you need to give at least one example of each category. In addition, you will frequently want to use linking words of **consequence** (or **result**) in the concluding sentence of a paragraph to summarize how your examples relate to your classification principle. Look at the following examples. Note the punctuation in each example.

Linking Words of Example

- *for example*

  Some of my friends are introspective and quiet people. *For example*, Ching and Hirofumi never say much when we are with other people.

- *for instance*

  People who live in the country are quite different from people who live in the city. My uncle, who is a farmer, is never in a hurry. Once, *for instance*, he spent the whole day sharpening all the knives in the house, a task that an impatient city person would have taken care of in an hour.

- *such as*

  Some service providers, *such as* doctors, lawyers, and professors, have great amounts of authority.

Linking Words of Consequence

- *therefore*

  I really enjoy the peaceful company of good friends. *Therefore*, I appreciate the serenity of both Carlos and Maria.

- *for this reason*

  Change makes life exciting; *for this reason*, life in a city is more appealing than life on a farm or in the suburbs for me.

- *as a result/consequence*

  The relationships between parents and children vary from one culture to another. *As a consequence*, parents' expectations of how their children will treat them when they get older vary as well.

- *consequently*

  More and more people who live alone adopt a pet for company. *Consequently*, the pet services industry has expanded greatly.

▶ *Practice 12* **Writing Sentences with Linking Words**

Combine the two ideas below with a linking word of example or of consequence. Watch your punctuation!

Example

sunny day—go swimming

It was a sunny day. Therefore, we went swimming.

1. miserable weather—cancel picnic

   _____

2. solar energy—heat water

   _____

3. being sick—going to the doctor

_____

4. former U.S. presidents—Bill Clinton

_____

5. too much work—not going to a party

_____

▶ *Writing To Communicate*

Now, it is your turn to write a classification essay. Choose one of these four topics. If none of them appeal to you, ask your teacher if you can choose a topic from "Other Essays" on pages 128–129.

1. Friends

Look back at Practice 7 on page 118. In that freewriting exercise, you classified your friends. Your subject is *my friends*.

Subject: _____ my friends _____

Now, write your principle of classification here:

Principle: _____

Write down your categories here:

Category 1: _____

Category 2: _____

Category 3: _____

Category 4: _____

Write a first draft of your essay. Make sure to support your categories by using examples, facts, or anecdotes to convince your reader that these categories are realistic.

2. Worrywarts, Bookworms, and Fatalists

Here is a second way to classify your friends. Look back at Practices 10 and 11 on pages 122 and 123. In Practice 10, you discussed the actions and characteristics of people who are worrywarts, bookworms, and fatalists. In Practice 11, you outlined an essay dividing your friends into these three categories.

3. My Family Characteristics

Look back at Practices 5 and 6 on pages 117 and 118. In Practice 5, you wrote about three kinds of traits in your family: appearance, interests, and skills. In Practice 6, you wrote a paragraph classifying those traits. Now you can expand those ideas and the paragraph you wrote into a complete essay.

Begin by thinking about your thesis statement. If you are going to use the three categories of appearance, interests, and skills, write a thesis statement that includes these.

Consider the examples or anecdotes you will use to support your thesis statement. For example, does your category of *appearance* include only such characteristics as height, or hair color, or the shape of your nose? Or are you also going to include such characteristics as the way you walk or sit and how you dress? If you use the categories of *interests* or *skills*, you will probably want to tell a brief story (anecdote) to illustrate that category.

Write an outline of your essay, making sure you include all the points you want to make. Then, expand your outline into an essay. Try to come up with an interesting introduction and conclusion.

4. Sports

Sports can be classified according to many principles. One principle could be the number of players needed. Another principle might be the equipment necessary. How many other principles can you think of to classify the subject *sports*?

Peer Help Worksheet

Check off each step as you complete it.

1 ▶ What did you find most interesting about this essay?

2 ▶ Organization

    a. How many body paragraphs does this essay have? _____ ... ❏

    b. Does the thesis statement show that there will be this number of
paragraphs? _____ Yes _____ No .... ❏

    c. Does each paragraph describe one category?

       _____ Yes _____ No .... ❏

       If the answer is No, write what you think the problem is: .... ❏

       _____

    d. Is there a conclusion? _____ Yes _____ No .... ❏

    e. If there is a conclusion, what kind is it? .... ❏

       _____

3 ▶ Editing

    a. Is all of the spelling correct? Underline all words that are
misspelled. Use a dictionary to correct the mistakes. .... ❏

    b. Are all of the commas correct? Circle any commas you think
are incorrect. Add any commas you think are missing. .... ❏

Other Essays

Look around you. Almost anything can be classified: trees, animals, chemicals, theories of government, and so on. Here are some other topics that lend themselves to a classification organizational pattern. Choose one and write an essay about it. Remember that giving concrete support by way of examples is very important in order to convince the reader that your classification is appropriate. Try to be as original as you can in your classifications to make the writing interesting for both you and the reader.

1. Look at movie listings, read some recent movie reviews, or go see a couple of movies. Then, write an essay classifying the subject *movies* into categories according to a principle (e.g., quality of acting, movie type, popularity). Use the titles of the movies as examples to support your classification and explain a little about each of the ones you use.

2. The number of jobs people can have seems endless, but many jobs have common features. Classify the subject *jobs* into a manageable number of categories—no more than five or six. Start by listing all the types of jobs you can think of; then, see if you can divide those into categories. What is your principle of classification? Write an essay that classifies these jobs.

3. All countries have a political system of organization; however, they also differ in the way their governments are set up. Think about and then list countries and their political systems. When you look at your list of countries, can you see a way of dividing them into categories? Use the principle of *political system*. How many categories do you find? Write an essay that explains your classification.

CHAPTER 13 Cause and Effect

▶

Raising Children

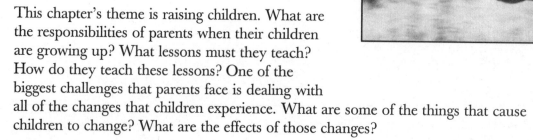

This chapter's theme is raising children. What are the responsibilities of parents when their children are growing up? What lessons must they teach? How do they teach these lessons? One of the biggest challenges that parents face is dealing with all of the changes that children experience. What are some of the things that cause children to change? What are the effects of those changes?

Of course, how a child is raised depends largely on the culture in which that child grows up. In some cultures, parents are very strict and give children lots of rules to follow. In other cultures, parents are encouraged to allow children to have more freedom. What about the culture in which you were raised? Did you grow up having a lot of rules or a lot of freedom? Compare your upbringing with your classmates'.

Prewriting

Analyzing a topic according to its causes and effects is often key to understanding it, and understanding a topic is, of course, the goal of any learning situation. Determining the causes and effects of an event, a scientific principle or a cultural practice isn't always as easy as it may seem. You need to be able to see both the immediate causes and their expected effects as well as the deeper causes and any unexpected results.

For example, consider the mother who arranges for her son to take piano lessons. What are the reasons for this? She may have many reasons, such as wanting to give her son an appreciation of music, a sense of discipline, or exposure to something new. A deeper reason, however, may be to give the son what the mother never had and, in this way, make a dream of her own come true. What will the effects of the piano lessons be? Ideally, they will be an appreciation of music as an adult and true enjoyment of playing. A parent's involvement may also have, and often does have, the opposite effect. In this case, the boy grows up to hate music and the piano because his mother forced him to take piano lessons.

> **What About You?**
>
> Did you learn to play a musical instrument when you were growing up? Who taught you? Did you enjoy it? Do you still play? If you didn't learn to play an instrument, do you wish you had?

▶ *Practice 1* Determining Causes and Effects

For each of these topics, identify the immediate and deep causes and the expected and unexpected effects. The first one has been done as an example.

Topic	Causes	Effects
Sending girls to girls-only or boys to boys-only high schools	immediate Girls and boys are too concerned with members of the opposite sex.	expected Girls and boys will concentrate more on their studies.
	deep Parents are afraid of their children becoming sexually active too early.	unexpected Girls and boys go behind their parent's backs to see members of the opposite sex.
Allowing a child to adopt a pet	immediate	expected
	deep	unexpected
Limiting the number of hours per week that a child can watch TV	immediate	expected
	deep	unexpected
Talking to teenagers about smoking, drinking alcohol, and using drugs	immediate	expected
	deep	unexpected

Graphic Organizers

The style of organization used for essays that analyze causes and effects is called **block**. There are several variations of this style. Look at the graphic organizer for block style 1. The writer has chosen to write about the causes and effects of getting a pet for a child. Note that one body paragraph explains the causes and the other explains the effects.

Block Style 1

Introductory paragraph

Thesis statement: While parents get pets for their children for obvious reasons, sometimes there are long-term results that can be surprising.

Body paragraph 1

Cause 1: The child is eager to have a pet.
Cause 2: The parents want to make their child happy.
Cause 3: The parents want to teach their child about responsibility.

Body paragraph 2

Effect 1: The child matures by accepting the responsibility of caring for a pet.
Effect 2: The child learns to get comfort from a nonparental source.
Effect 3: The child develops a feeling of compassion for a living creature other than himself or herself.

Concluding paragraph

Another variation of the block style is to talk only about the causes of a situation. You might choose to do this if you want to discuss and explain the causes in more detail.

Block Style 2

Introductory paragraph

Thesis statement: Parents get a pet for their child for many reasons.

Body paragraph 1

Cause 1: The child is eager to have a pet.

Body paragraph 2
Cause 2: The parents want to make their child happy.

Body paragraph 3
Cause 3: The parents want to teach their child about responsibility.

Concluding paragraph

Similarly, you might want to analyze only the effects of a situation; in this case, your body paragraphs will discuss in detail each effect that you have identified. This is the third variation of the block style of organization.

Block Style 3

Introductory paragraph
Thesis statement: There are many beneficial effects of a child having a pet.

Body paragraph 1
Effect 1: The child matures by accepting the responsibility of caring for a pet.

Body paragraph 2
Effect 2: The child learns to get comfort from a nonparental source.

Body paragraph 2
Effect 3: The child develops a feeling of compassion for a living creature other than himself or herself.

Concluding paragraph

Freewriting

▶ *Practice 2* **Writing about Effects**

Draw a line down the middle of a piece of paper. Think about your upbringing, and, on the right side of the page, quickly write down some decisions your parents made for you that have greatly affected your life. Then, on the left side, write down why you think your parents made those decisions. You may want to refer back to this assignment when you are writing your cause-and-effect essay later in the chapter.

Model Essays

Read the model cause-and-effect essays that follow.

Model Essay 1 ———————————————————————————

Growing Up with Rules

It is said that for every action, there is a reaction. That saying is perfectly illustrated by the way that my parents disciplined my brothers and sisters and me. To me, it was an ordinary family, but I later learned that having ten children was anything but ordinary. It required a certain number of rules, and my parents were not shy about making those rules. The rules in our house were strict and had both short-term and long-term effects.

First of all, from the time we were very young, we were responsible for keeping our rooms neat and clean. Our parents did a daily "inspection" of our rooms that could occur at any time. If our beds were not made or our clothes were not hung up or our toys were left out, we were immediately taken to our rooms when we got home from school and told to correct the situation. When we didn't keep our rooms clean, we had to help my mom for the rest of the afternoon instead of going out and playing with friends. Therefore, in fact, we kept our rooms fairly tidy, and we got to like them like that. As adults, I think we all can now appreciate this discipline of tidying up before leaving our rooms, apartments, or houses.

Doing as well as possible in school was also very important in our family. Homework time began right after dinner, and each child was required to explain to one or both parents what he or she was doing. Asking for help was permitted, but being lazy was not. When we were caught daydreaming instead of doing our homework, the punishment was quick and certain: no TV for a week. Good grades were not necessarily expected, but making a good effort was. If one of our teachers contacted my parents with a discipline problem or with a simple comment that one of us wasn't working up to our abilities, we all got a lecture from my parents about what our responsibilities as children were. Today, my parents can boast that all ten of their children are college graduates and that among them are two doctors and two college professors.

Finally, our parents always made sure that we understood how important our relationships to each other were. We were taught to love and respect our siblings because they were the only people that we would always be able to count on. From a very early age, we learned to share what we had with each other. Later, we learned to support each other through hard times at school or around the neighborhood. We would stick together like glue if one of us were in trouble or threatened. In my family, the result of our not caring for each other was the look of such profound disappointment in my parents' eyes that it would break our hearts. Our parents always forgave us in the end; nevertheless, it was a terrible feeling. The long-term result of this is that we are all very close today.

Some people think my upbringing was rather strict and even cruel, but I do not. As an adult, I live in an orderly home, am very happy working in my chosen profession as a college professor, and have no better friends than my brothers and sisters. I believe I owe my parents and their rules for the stability and contentment I have in my life.

| tidy: neat | to boast: to speak about something proudly | siblings: brothers and sisters |
| | | profound: strong, serious, deep |

▶ *Practice 3*   Questions about "Growing Up with Rules"

Answer the following questions.

1. What is the thesis statement?

   _____

2. Which organizational pattern is used? Block style 1, 2, or 3?

   _____

3. How many causes are discussed?

   _____

4. How many effects are discussed? What type? Short-term? Long-term?

   _____

Model Essay 2

Rebels with Causes and Effects

The anthropologist Margaret Mead is well known for her studies of adolescents in various societies, particularly primitive ones. She believes that the transition from child to adult does not always have to be a difficult one. Nevertheless, it seems to be full of problems in many Western societies. In the United States, for example, going through the teenage years is challenging for both teenagers and their parents. We can take comfort, however, in the fact that there are many reasons that teenagers rebel against their parents and in the fact that there are also positive effects.

Probably the most primitive reason for teenage rebelliousness is physical in nature. At about the beginning of adolescence, children are undergoing profound hormonal changes as their bodies go through puberty. Their bodies are telling them that they are no longer children, and yet their parents are still treating them as children. Psychologically, they need to distance themselves from their parents to establish themselves as adults, and this psychological distance is accompanied by physical distance. At the same time, teenagers want to become more like their friends, so everything that has to do with their parents must be avoided. In fact, often parents represent "the establishment" and, in the extreme, all the evil that it has created in the world.

There do seem to be benefits to this difficult time, however. While teenagers are going through this rebellious period, they are also learning to think for themselves and to evaluate the world around them. They are becoming socialized and independent from their families. They are forming relationships outside the family, which is very important if they are going to survive as individuals. The experimentation of this period is also important as long as it is not taken to extremes. By experimenting, teenagers gain experience and the confidence that comes with it. Ultimately, the teenager reaches adulthood with the social and psychological strength it takes to become a productive member of society.

In conclusion, despite the difficulty and awkwardness of adolescence, it is a necessary step in creating responsible, thinking adults. In addition, while teenagers and parents alike may not think that they will get through it, most do. In fact, they are usually better and stronger people because of it.

an anthropologist: a scientist who studies people and their cultures	**profound**: strong, serious, deep	**"the establishment"**: the organizations and people in a society who have a lot of power and who are opposed to new ideas
an adolescent: a teenager	**puberty**: the stage of physical development when children begin to mature sexually (usually at twelve or thirteen years old)	
hormonal: having to do with body chemicals that influence growth and development		**extreme**: the greatest, farthest point away

 Practice 4   Questions about "Rebels with Causes and Effects"

Answer the following questions.

1. What is the thesis statement?

   _____

2. Which organizational pattern is used? Block style 1, 2, or 3?

   _____

3. How many causes are discussed?

   _____

4. How many effects are discussed? What type? Short-term? Long-term?

The Introductory Paragraph in the Cause-and-Effect Essay

When you use block style 2 or 3 for essays in which you discuss only the causes or only the effects, an ideal approach to the introductory paragraph presents itself. This approach is to talk briefly about the effects if the essay discusses only the causes or, conversely, talk briefly about the causes if the essay discusses the effects. Look again at this outline:

Block Style 2: Causes Only

Thesis statement: Parents get a pet for their child for many reasons.

Cause 1: The child is eager to have a pet.

Cause 2: The parents want to make their child happy.

Cause 3: The parents want to teach their child about responsibility.

With this essay, it is possible to write an introductory paragraph that briefly discusses the effects. For example:

Many parents are at some point faced with the question of whether or not to get their child a pet. Almost all children love the idea of having a dog or a cat or even a turtle or a fish. Children who have such experiences benefit later in life when they are able to get comfort from someone outside their family and are able to show concern for people less fortunate than themselves. These benefits usually come from very simple beginnings. In fact, parents get their child pets for many simple reasons.

▶ *Practice 5*   Writing an Introductory Paragraph

Read the following outline for an essay that discusses only the effects of children having a pet. Write an introductory paragraph that briefly discusses the causes. Use the thesis statement given.

Block Style 3: Effects Only

Thesis statement: There are many beneficial effects of a child having a pet.

Effect 1: The child matures by accepting the responsibility of caring for a pet.

Effect 2: The child learns to get comfort from a nonparental source.

Effect 3: The child develops a feeling of compassion for a living creature other than himself or herself.

Linking Words of Cause and Effect

The following chart lists common linking words for connecting two ideas in a cause-and-effect relationship.

	Transitions	Conjunctions		Prepositions
		Subordinating	Coordinating	
Cause		because since as now that	for	because of due to
Effect	as a result consequently therefore as a consequence for this reason hence thus		so	

One of the ways to make your writing more sophisticated is to vary your sentence structures. A simple way of doing this is to use the four types of linking words to combine ideas. Look at these various ways to combine two ideas:

Transitions

Many Web sites are inappropriate for children. *Therefore*, parents should monitor their children's computer time.

Many Web sites are inappropriate for children; *for this reason*, parents should monitor their children's computer time.

Subordinating Conjunctions

Because many Web sites are inappropriate for children, parents should monitor their children's computer time.

Parents should monitor their children's computer time *since* many Web sites are inappropriate for children.

Coordinating Conjunctions

Many Web sites are inappropriate for children, *so* parents should monitor their children's computer time.

Parents should monitor their children's computer time, *for* many Web sites are inappropriate for children.

Prepositions

When you use a preposition to combine two sentences, you must change the sentence that follows the preposition into a noun phrase, since prepositions are always followed by nouns. There are three ways to do this:

1. Use the noun form of an adjective:

> *Due to* the <u>inappropriateness</u> for children of many Web sites, parents should monitor their children's computer time.

2. Use *the fact that* and the entire sentence:

> *Due to* <u>the fact that</u> many Web sites are inappropriate for children, parents should monitor their children's computer time.

3. Use the gerund form of the verb:

> *Due to* many Web sites' <u>being</u> inappropriate for children, parents should monitor their children's computer time.

▶ *Practice 6* **Combining Sentences**

Combine the sets of sentences using the linking word in parentheses. Make any changes necessary, but do not change the meaning of the sentences. The first one is done as an example.

1. Playing sports after school is good for children. It promotes a sense of teamwork.

    (*because*) <u>Playing sports after school is good for children because it</u>
    <u>promotes a sense of teamwork.</u>

    (*consequently*) _____

    _____

    (*so*) _____

    _____

    (*due to*) _____

    _____

2. Teenagers sometimes lie to their parents. They don't want to be punished.

    (*as a result*) _____

    _____

    (*as*) _____

    _____

    (*because of*) _____

    _____

3. The decision to have a baby is very important. It should be given a lot of thought.

(*since*) _____

_____

(*due to*) _____

_____

(*so*) _____

_____

▶ Writing To Communicate

Now, it is your turn to write a cause-and-effect essay. Choose one of these three topics. If none of them appeal to you, ask your teacher if you can choose a topic from "Other Essays" on page 144.

1. Who Am I?

It is widely believed that people's identities come from their genetic makeup and their environment. Write an essay about the environmental reasons that make you the person you are. In other words, to which people or to what experiences do you owe some of your traits and characteristics?

- food likes and dislikes

- hobbies (including sports/exercise)

- religious beliefs

- holiday observances and rituals

- fears and superstitions

- housekeeping (e.g., messy or tidy)

- personality type (e.g., optimist or pessimist, introvert or extrovert, people-person or loner, etc.)

- qualities desired in a life partner

- weather/natural environment preferences

- sense of humor

2. Bringing Up Baby

Like just about everything, raising a child differs from culture to culture. The principles that a particular culture has about raising children will have a variety of causes and effects. Write an essay that analyzes the principles of raising children in your culture in terms of their causes and/or effects. Consider the following:

- cultural morals

- religion

- education

- discipline and punishment

- responsibilities of the parent to the child

- responsibilities of the child to the parent

3. Choosing a School for Your Child

Today in the United States, parents can choose among many different types of schools for their children. Look at the information about these five elementary schools, choose the one that you think would be best for your child, and write an essay that explains why you would send a child of yours to that school.

School Choice 1: Central School, a public school

- *Philosophy:* to provide a well-rounded education for boys and girls in order to produce productive citizens
- *Acceptance criterion:* residence in the district
- *Curriculum:* standard, state-issued; stresses academic subjects of English, arithmetic, and science; no nonacademic skills taught
- *Scores of school graduates on standardized tests:* average
- *Extracurricular activities:* after-school sports for boys and girls
- *Student–teacher ratio:* 32:1
- *Cost:* none to parents (paid for with local taxes)

School Choice 2: Belmont School, a private Montessori school

- *Philosophy:* to develop initiative and self-reliance in boys and girls by letting them set their own pace and way for learning
- *Acceptance criteria*: none
- *Curriculum:* no set curriculum that is covered from day to day because children learn at their own pace. Teachers guide students to increasingly more complex tasks as they express interest in them.
- *Scores of school graduates on standardized tests:* above average
- *Extracurricular activities:* nothing is considered extra-curricular
- *Student–teacher ratio:* 20:1
- *Cost:* $12,000 per year

School Choice 3: Coastside School, a public alternative school

- *Philosophy:* to develop boys' and girls' skills in music, art, and drama
- *Acceptance criterion*: students must demonstrate a talent in a particular area as a condition of acceptance into the school
- *Curriculum:* minimum work on academic subjects, such as English, mathematics, and science; most students' time is spent developing their special talent
- *Scores of school graduates on standardized tests:* slightly below average, especially for math and science
- *Extracurricular activities:* none
- *Student–teacher ratio:* 36:1 in academic courses; 16:1 in others

- *Cost:* none for the classes (paid for with local taxes), but several thousand dollars for the equipment needed for the student's specialty

School 4: Holy School, a private religious school

- *Philosophy:* to provide a well-rounded education for boys and girls and to instill in them religious values

- *Acceptance criterion:* none, but parents are encouraged to be active participants in the religion

- *Curriculum:* standard, state-issued; stresses academic subjects of English, arithmetic, and science; some fine arts classes and a religion class every day

- *Scores of school graduates on standardized tests:* slightly above average

- *Extracurricular activities:* after-school sports for boys and girls; mandatory religion classes and activities on the weekend

- *Student–teacher ratio:* 20:1

- *Cost:* $10,000 per year

School 5: Ocean School, a private alternative school

- *Philosophy:* to provide a well-rounded education for boys and girls; Ocean School believes that single-sex classes can best attain this goal, so boys and girls are separated; the boys' school is on the north side of the street, and the girls' school is on the south side of the street

- *Acceptance criteria:* none

- *Curriculum:* standard, state-issued; stresses academic subjects of English, arithmetic, and science; some nonacademic classes, such as music and dance for girls and woodshop and auto mechanics for boys

- *Scores of school graduates on standardized tests:* well above average for girls; somewhat above average for boys

- *Extracurricular activities:* after-school sports for boys and girls

- *Student–teacher ratio:* 20:1

- *Cost:* $10,000 per year

Peer Help Worksheet

Check off each step as you complete it.

1 ▶ What did you particularly like about this essay?

2 ▶ Content:

    a. Is the essay clear? Which parts were especially clear? . . . . ❏

    b. Are there parts of the essay that aren't as clear?
       Which parts? . . . . ❏

3 ▶ Organization:

    a. What is the thesis statement? Does it represent what
       is in the essay's body paragraphs? . . . . ❏

    b. How is the thesis statement introduced in the introductory
       paragraph? (Check one.)

       With an anecdote . . . . ❏
       With facts or statistics . . . . ❏
       With a bit of history . . . . ❏
       By going from the general to the specific . . . . ❏
       By talking about the effects . . . . ❏
       By talking about the causes . . . . ❏

    c. Which type of cause-and-effect organizational pattern
       does it use? (Check one.)

       Block style 1 . . . . ❏
       Block style 2 . . . . ❏
       Block style 3 . . . . ❏
       Unclear . . . . ❏

    d. If the style is unclear, explain how it is so. _____
       _____ . . . . ❏

    e. How many causes are discussed? _____ How many
       effects? _____ . . . . ❏

    f. Which components of a concluding paragraph does this
       concluding paragraph have? (Check all that apply.)

       A restatement of the thesis statement . . . . ❏
       A summary of the body paragraphs . . . . ❏
       A final comment . . . . ❏

4 ▶ Editing

    a. Are the punctuation patterns used correctly? Check all the
       linking words that are used in the essay. . . . . ❏

    b. Is there a variety in the type of punctuation patterns used? . . . . . ❏

Other Essays

Here are some other topics that lend themselves to a cause-and-effect organizational pattern. Choose one and write an essay about it.

1. We have all had people who inspire us to be the very best that we can by teaching us or by simply being an example for us to follow. These people are called *mentors*. Mentors are special because they help people not because they necessarily have to, but because they want to. Who has been a mentor in your life so far? Write an essay that explains why this person has affected you so much.

2. There are many areas in the world that are in varying states of political, social, or economic unrest. Choose an area that you are familiar with and write an essay that explains the causes and/or effects of the unrest. Consider these points:

    *   What is the history of the region? Does the history affect the present?

    *   Is there one person or one group of people behind the unrest?

    *   What has the reaction of the average person been? How has the unrest affected people's daily lives?

3. It seems the environment is in a lot of danger these days. There have been some victories in terms of saving and preserving it, but it seems there still is a long way to go. Choose a particularly difficult environmental problem that is prevalent in your country and discuss some of the effects on the people living there. Some examples are:

    *   overpopulation

    *   pollution

    *   species extinction

    *   disappearing rain forests

    *   disappearing natural resources

4. History is full of cause-and-effect relationships. Choose one historical event in your country's history and explain the reasons for it and the effects of it.

CHAPTER 14 Comparison and Contrast

▶

People and Nature

Our natural surroundings play a big part in the way we live. In mountainous areas, people have a difficult time traveling, so towns often get quite isolated. In hot climates, people build houses that keep out the sun, and they plant plenty of trees for shade. The reverse is also true in that people influence nature by the way they build, manufacture, and travel. This chapter's theme is how nature affects people and how people affect nature. Discuss these questions with your classmates.

- Is the city or town where you live now different from the one in which you grew up? How is it different?

- Where would you rather live: in the countryside or in a city? Why?

- Is the natural environment of your home country similar throughout the country, or are some areas very different from others? Do you think this difference in environment influences how people think and behave in those areas?

Prewriting

Comparing and contrasting are very common in academic writing. The purpose of a **comparison** is to show how people, places, things, or ideas are similar, and the purpose of **contrast** is to show how people, places, things, or ideas are different. For example, in a computer science class, you may be asked to compare two programming languages. In a literature class, your professor may ask you to compare two novels. In a political science class, your assignment may be to contrast two or more theories of economics. Since comparative writing can get quite complex, it is critical to pay attention to your organization. In this chapter, you will study how to organize comparison-and-contrast essays to communicate your ideas clearly and concisely.

▶ *Practice 1*   Comparing Two Houses

In this exercise, you will "build" two houses for two different families. Look at this list of characteristics:

1. 1,200 square feet
2. 2 bedrooms, 1 bathroom
3. 2,000 square feet
4. 3 bedrooms, 3 bathrooms
5. indoor palm trees in pots
6. abstract paintings
7. built of wood
8. curtains in every window
9. front door with glass panes
10. faces a busy street
11. grass hasn't been cut in a month
12. gray carpet, red chairs, bright blue rug
13. large, messy garden
14. lots of flowering indoor plants
15. made of brick
16. old oak door
17. set back from the street
18. 1 level
19. small brick patio
20. soft beige couch and chairs
21. very little furniture, no clutter
22. 2 levels
23. wood floor
24. security light above the entry door

Organize the characteristics into two imaginary houses. There will be twelve characteristics for each house. Cross off each characteristic as you write it under one house or the other.

House 1

Size and building materials

_____

_____

_____

_____

The outside of the house

_____

_____

_____

_____

Furniture and decoration

_____

_____

_____

_____

House 2

Size and building materials

_____

_____

_____

_____

The outside of the house

_____

_____

_____

_____

Furniture and decoration

_____

_____

_____

Now, imagine two families, the Noors and the Jacksons. Mr. and Mrs. Noor are a retired couple in their seventies whose grandchildren come to visit a couple of times each month. The Jackson family consists of a single father and his two teenage children. Which family would you place in each house? Take notes below, then discuss with your classmates and present your reasoning to the class.

Family in House 1: _____

Why? _____

_____

_____

_____

_____

_____

Family in House 2: _____

Why? _____

_____

_____

_____

_____

_____

▶ *Practice 2*   **Comparing People**

Look at these photographs of two young men. Create an imaginary life for each of them. Write their names under the photos. Then write some of their characteristics under the names.

Name: _____   Name: _____

Age: _____   Age: _____

Nationality: _____   Nationality: _____

Education: _____   Education: _____

Work experience: _____   Work experience: _____

_____   _____

_____   _____

Interests, hobbies: _____   Interests, hobbies: _____

_____   _____

_____   _____

Skills: _____   Skills: _____

_____   _____

_____   _____

Future plans: _____   Future plans: _____

_____   _____

_____   _____

Are the two men mostly similar or mostly different? If you were to write an essay about them, would you focus on their similarities or their differences? Did your classmates imagine very different lives for either one of the men? Discuss the similarities and the differences.

Graphic Organizers

There are basically three ways of organizing essays that use the comparison and contrast rhetorical pattern. The first style first introduces the similarities between two objects and then the differences, or vice versa. This is called the **basic block style**.

Basic Block Style

Introductory paragraph
Thesis statement

Body paragraph 1: Differences between the two houses

- Size and building materials
- Furniture and decoration
- The outside of the houses

Body paragraph 2: Similarities between the two houses

- Single-family houses
- Indoor plants
- Outside yard or patio

Concluding paragraph

Below is the second organizational style, which also has two body paragraphs. However, in this style, you describe one item completely in the first body paragraph, and in the second body paragraph you describe the second item. It is important to note that in the second body paragraph, you need to show how the second item compares with the first one. We call this the **block comparison style**.

Block Comparison Style

Introductory paragraph
Thesis statement

Body paragraph 1: Description of House 1

- Size and building materials
- Furniture and decoration
- The outside of the house

```
┌─────────────────────────────────────────────────────────────┐
│                                                               │
│       Body paragraph 2: Description of House 2 compared with House 1 │
│                                                               │
│     • Size and building materials                             │
│         * difference in size                                  │
│         * difference in number of levels                      │
│         * etc.                                                │
│     • Furniture and decoration                                │
│         * difference in furniture style                       │
│         * similarity in having indoor plants                  │
│         * etc.                                                │
│     • The outside of the house                                │
│         * difference in location and entry doors              │
│         * similarity in having a yard or patio                │
│         * etc.                                                │
│                                                               │
└─────────────────────────────────────────────────────────────┘

┌─────────────────────────────────────────────────────────────┐
│                    Concluding paragraph                       │
└─────────────────────────────────────────────────────────────┘
```

The third style of organizing a comparison and contrast essay is called **point-by-point comparison**. In this style, you will have several body paragraphs. In fact, you will have as many body paragraphs as you have points of comparison. In this example, there are three body paragraphs about the two houses.

Point-by-Point Comparison Style

```
┌─────────────────────────────────────────────────────────────┐
│                    Introductory paragraph                     │
│                                                               │
│                     Thesis statement                          │
└─────────────────────────────────────────────────────────────┘

┌─────────────────────────────────────────────────────────────┐
│      Body paragraph 1: First point of comparison of the two houses │
│                                                               │
│     • Size and building materials                             │
│         * square footage                                      │
│         * number of rooms                                     │
│         * etc.                                                │
└─────────────────────────────────────────────────────────────┘

┌─────────────────────────────────────────────────────────────┐
│     Body paragraph 2: Second point of comparison of the two houses │
│                                                               │
│     • Furniture and decoration                                │
│         * floors                                              │
│         * furniture                                           │
│         * indoor plants                                       │
│         * etc.                                                │
└─────────────────────────────────────────────────────────────┘
```

Body paragraph 3: Third point of comparison of the two houses

- The outside of the houses
    * garden or patio
    * entry doors
    * street
    * etc.

Concluding paragraph

▶ *Practice 3* Choosing an Organizational Pattern

Look at Practice 2 on page 148. If you were writing an essay in which you first described one man and then described the second man and how he compared to the first man, which of the three organizational patterns would you use?

_____ Basic block   _____ Block comparison   _____ Point-by-point comparison

▶ *Practice 4* Outlining an Essay in Basic Block

Reorganize the descriptions of the two men into a pattern where you first describe their similarities and then examine their differences. [*Note*: If you find that you have very few similarities, you may have to change some of the characteristics of one of the men.]

Write down their names:

Man 1: _____   Man 2: _____

Write your essay outline here or on a piece of paper if you need more space.

   I. Introductory paragraph with thesis statement

   II. Body paragraph 1

        Similarities between _____ and _____

        First similarity: _____

        Second similarity: _____

        Third similarity: _____

        _____

        _____

        _____

III. Body paragraph 2

Differences between _____ and _____

First difference: _____

Second difference: _____

Third difference: _____

_____

_____

IV. Concluding paragraph

Freewriting

 Practice 5 **Then and Now**

The topic of this practice is "My Life as a Child and My Life Today." Think back to when you were five, seven, or ten years old. What were your dreams and interests? How did you see yourself? Have these dreams, interests, and thoughts about yourself changed since then? Write about the similarities and differences between you as a child and you now. Don't worry about organization, accuracy, or style. You may want to refer back to this assignment when you are writing your comparison-and-contrast essay later in the chapter.

Model Essays

Read the model comparison-and-contrast essays that follow.

Model Essay 1 ——————————————————————

A Tale of Two Towns

"Where do you come from?" is a question many Americans can't answer easily. Many Americans were born in one place, lived a few years in another, went to elementary school in a third town, and so on. In my home country, we usually live all our lives in the town where we were born, but my family is different. We moved from one small town to another when I was twelve years old. For this reason, I have two "hometowns." Although the people in the two towns think that they have nothing in common, in my opinion, they have far more similarities than differences.

The first obvious similarity lies in the location of the two towns. They are both seaside towns, lying on the south coast of Norway. They are sheltered from the ocean storms by a large group of islands and backed by hills that defend them against the cold winter winds. There are a few minor differences in their location, of course: Kristiansand, my childhood city, spreads out onto many of the protecting islands, while Arendal, my teenage town, is small and isn't as well protected.

Second, both Kristiansand and Arendal are small. Compared to the great continental cities of Paris and Rome, they are not even dots on a map. Kristiansand is a little larger with 40,000 inhabitants, while Arendal has only about 35,000, but neither can be called a metropolis.

Furthermore, at least to a visitor, they are quite similar in their natural beauty. The islands are rough and rocky. The houses of both towns are mostly small, white-painted wooden buildings, and the vegetation is almost exactly the same in both towns: birch trees, a few fir trees, low bushes, and moss. In addition, the ocean is a major influence on the lifestyle of both towns, and the weather forecast is the major topic of conversation.

The economies of the two towns are also based on the same business: tourism. Both native Norwegians and foreigners go on summer vacation to the two towns, and in winter, business is very slow. Of course, there are a few differences here as well. In Arendal, there are still several fishermen making a living from the sea, while Kristiansand is a busy port for large commercial ships. Still, I doubt that either town could support the population it has without the tourists.

Finally, despite the opinions of the natives of Kristiansand and Arendal, I think that the people there are very similar. Because of the size of the towns, people are mostly interested in what their neighbors do and say, and they don't care very much about what is happening in the outside world. In addition, the inhabitants of the two towns have a love–hate relationship with the necessary tourists. These tourists bring in business and money in the summer, so the natives smile at them when they meet them. However, behind their backs, the townspeople wish that they would just spend their money and go home.

Thus, while there *are* a few differences between Arendal and Kristiansand, I think that the similarities are by far more obvious. In location, size, natural beauty, economy, and people, they are very much alike. Although I sometimes feel they are too small for me now, they are my hometowns, and there is no place like home.

> **What About You?**
>
> Think about two cities you know. What are the first points of comparison that come to mind? Perhaps you think of their locations, cultural attractions, or shopping districts. What are other ways to compare these two cities?

a tale: a story	**a birch tree**: a tree with a white trunk and small leaves	**to make a living from**: to get their income from
to have nothing in common: to be very different from each other	**a fir tree**: a tree with leaves shaped like needles that do not fall off in winter	**a port**: a place where ships can load and unload people or things
to shelter: to protect		
a metropolis: a very large city	**moss**: a small, flat green plant that looks like fur and often grows on trees and rocks	
vegetation: plants, especially all the plants in one particular area		

▶ *Practice 6*   Questions about "A Tale of Two Towns"

Answer the following questions.

1. What is being compared in this essay?

   _____ People   _____ Towns   _____ The writer's childhood

2. What are the topics of the five body paragraphs of this essay?

   _____

   _____

   _____

   _____

   _____

3. What is the organizational pattern of this essay?

   ____ Basic block   ____ Block comparison   ____ Point-by-point comparison

4. How many differences are there? How many similarities?

   Differences: _____   Similarities: _____

Model Essay 2

My Two Sisters

My grandfather, who was interested in genealogy, once traced our family tree as far back as he could, but he couldn't get farther back than 1759. In that year, a foreign ship visited my family's little fishing village, and nine months later, the only daughter in that family had a baby boy. No one knows what nationality that sailor was, but the genes he passed on have been playing tricks with our family ever since. In every generation, someone shows up who is radically different from all the others. In my generation, it's my older sister, Lisa, who is different. Lisa and Ellen, who is my other sister, are as opposite as night and day.

Lisa typifies the radically different part of the family. Lisa is tall, slim, and elegant, with long dark hair and brown eyes. She looks tanned even in winter and is always the first person in spring to start wearing shorts. Her personality fits her looks. When Lisa gets angry, she doesn't just do it in a small way; she makes such a commotion that it can be heard in the next town. When she's happy, she's ecstatic. When Lisa found out that she had passed her university entrance exam, she danced in bare feet through the whole town and partied for two solid weeks. She is always on the lookout for new and exciting experiences, and she never does anything halfheartedly. Her passion for life extends from love to politics; she's divorced with three daughters by two different husbands, and she's a dedicated socialist. There's nothing ordinary about Lisa.

Ellen, my younger sister, is her exact opposite. Where Lisa is tall and dark, Ellen is short (5 feet, 2 inches) and blond. Lisa wears her hair long and loose, but Ellen has no time for such nonsense and wears her blond hair in a short, practical style. Ellen's eyes are summer-sky blue, clear and untroubled. In summer, Lisa tans, but Ellen gets sunburned easily and always carries bottles of suntan lotion for herself and her equally blond children. Ellen is as calm as Lisa is excitable. I have never yet heard her raise her voice at anyone, and her laugh is a gentle breeze in contrast to Lisa's hurricane. Unlike Lisa, Ellen has never changed husbands, nor does she have any intention of doing so. On her wedding day, Ellen smiled softly and dressed in a traditional white dress. Lisa, on the other hand, wore a red mini-dress at her first wedding and blue jeans at her second. Ellen is a summer day, a calm ocean. She devotes herself entirely to her children and her house. Visiting Ellen's house is like coming home.

How can two such opposites be born to the same family? Until genetic research can come up with an answer, I am content to believe the story of the unknown sailor. In fact, even if a scientist should find the real answer, I'd rather not know. Some things are more interesting when they are left to the imagination.

What About You?

In Chapter 12, you described your family traits, focusing on the similarities among the people in your family. Now think about your differences. How are you different from your mother or your father?

---

genealogy: the study of a family's history

to trace: to study the history or development of something

genes: parts of cells that control the qualities that are passed to a living thing from its parents

commotion: sudden, noisy activity

ecstatic: very happy and excited

halfheartedly: without trying or wanting to be successful

practical: sensible, useful

a hurricane: a very bad storm that has strong, fast winds

Answer the following questions.

1. What is being compared in this essay?

   _____ People   _____ Genealogy   _____ Fashions   _____ Families

2. What are the topics of the two body paragraphs of this essay?

   Body paragraph 1: _____

   Body paragraph 2: _____

3. What is the organizational pattern of this essay?

   _____ Basic block   _____ Block comparison   _____ Point-by-point comparison

4. List the points of comparison between Lisa and Ellen. The first one has been done for you.

   _____ *Physical description* _____

   _____

   _____

Model Essay 3 ──────────────────────────────────

The Working Life

I have held six part-time jobs so far, and I have learned something from each one of them. I had my first paid job during the summer vacation before I started high school, picking strawberries at a farm near our summerhouse. During three of my four high school years, I cleaned offices near my house once a week after school. I have also worked as a receptionist for a passenger ferry company, a salesperson in a clothing store, a math tutor for middle school students, and a maid in a hotel. While there are a few similarities between these jobs, I think the differences between them are much greater.

One obvious similarity is that they have all been part time. My parents didn't allow me to work more than one evening and one of the weekend days (Saturday or Sunday) while I was a student. Of course, I often worked full time for a month or so during the summer but never during the school year. Another similarity is that they were all basically entry-level, unskilled positions. One might think that being a math tutor was a more highly skilled job, but actually I was given all the assignments and detailed directions for how to teach the math points by the school. Still, I think the differences between these jobs are much more striking than the similarities.

The first big difference between them was the amount of mental and physical work involved. My two jobs as a strawberry picker and as a hotel maid involved a lot of heavy lifting, and in both of them I walked many miles every day. I remember crying after my second day in the strawberry field because my back muscles were so sore. The office cleaning job did involve some physical work, such as moving chairs and wastebaskets, but it was very easy in comparison. For my receptionist, tutor, and salesperson jobs, I worked in air-conditioned comfort and never lifted anything heavier than a pencil or a dress. Second, there was a great difference in the amount of independence I had. Picking strawberries, I could go as slowly or as quickly as I wanted; the more strawberries I picked, the more money I got. As a salesperson, I was also paid a commission on the amount I sold, so I had a lot of independence. In my other four jobs, I was told exactly what to do and when to do it. However, the biggest difference, in my opinion, was whether the work involved people or objects. When you are picking fruit and cleaning offices or hotel rooms, you really don't need to talk with people much. Sometimes a whole day could go by in those jobs when I hardly said anything to anyone, but as a receptionist, salesperson, or tutor, establishing pleasant and effective relationships with other people was critical.

To summarize, the similarities in the amount of work and the level of skill needed are not nearly as obvious as the differences between these jobs. Physical labor is hard on your body, but the hardest thing about these jobs for me was that I rarely got to talk with anyone. I love to talk, and I have discovered that I need to have independence and responsibility in the kind of work I do. As a result, I kept my part-time salesperson job through all four years of high school. Being a receptionist was somewhat boring, but at least I got to chat with a lot of different people. Therefore, besides earning pocket money and saving for college and some vacations abroad, my six jobs have taught me a lot about the kind of work that suits me. A career with lots of independence, responsibility, and interaction with interesting people is the path for me.

What About You?

What was your first paid job? Did you like it? What did you learn from it?

a ferry: a boat that travels regularly from one port to another, usually carrying people	**entry-level**: for someone with no experience	**a commission**: payment that varies depending on how much you do or sell
a tutor: a private teacher for a single person or a small group	**to be sore**: to have muscles that hurt	**to chat**: to talk in a friendly, informal way

▶ *Practice 8*   Questions about "The Working Life"

Answer the following questions.

1. What is being compared in this essay?

    _____ People   _____ Jobs   _____ Physical labor

2. What are the topics of the two body paragraphs of this essay?

    Body paragraph 1: _____

    Body paragraph 2: _____

3. What is the organizational pattern of this essay?

_____ Basic block   _____ Block comparison   _____ Point-by-point comparison

4. List the similarities and differences between jobs as they are described in this essay.

Similarities:

_____

_____

_____

Differences:

_____

_____

_____

Concluding Paragraphs

In Chapter 9, you practiced writing concluding paragraphs. Remember that a concluding paragraph can be a summary, a restatement of the thesis statement, a final comment on the topic, or a combination of these.

▶ *Practice 9*   **Analyzing Concluding Paragraphs**

The concluding paragraphs from the three model essays in this chapter have been repeated below. Which of the mechanisms have been used in these essay conclusions? Remember that more than one can apply.

Model Essay 1: A Tale of Two Towns

Thus, while there *are* a few differences between Arendal and Kristiansand, I think that the similarities are by far more obvious. In location, size, natural beauty, economy, and people, they are very much alike. Although I sometimes feel they are too small for me now, they are my hometowns, and there is no place like home.

_____ Summary   _____ Restatement   _____ Final comment

Model Essay 2: My Two Sisters

How can two such opposites be born to the same family? Until genetic research can come up with an answer, I am content to believe the story of the unknown sailor. In fact, even if a scientist should find the real answer, I'd rather not know. Some things are more interesting when they are left to the imagination.

_____ Summary   _____ Restatement   _____ Final comment

Model Essay 3: The Working Life

To summarize, the similarities in the amount of work and the level of skill needed are not nearly as obvious as the differences between these jobs. Physical labor is hard on your body, but the hardest thing about these jobs for me was that I rarely got to talk with anyone. I love to talk, and I have discovered that I need to have independence and responsibility in the kind of work I do. As a result, I kept my part-time salesperson job both through all four years of high school. Being a receptionist was somewhat boring, but at least I got to chat with a lot of different people. Therefore, besides earning pocket money and saving for college and some vacations abroad, my six jobs have taught me a lot about the kind of work that suits me. A career with lots of independence, responsibility, and interaction with interesting people is the path for me.

_____ Summary   _____ Restatement   _____ Final comment

Linking Words and Punctuation

Linking Words

Linking words of comparison and contrast are of the three types: **transitions**, **conjunctions**, and **prepositions** and **prepositional phrases**. Here are examples of their use in comparing the two imaginary towns: "Stonecreek" and "Linden."

Showing Differences

Transitions

1. Linden is exciting. *On the other hand*, Stonecreek is dull.

2. Stonecreek is dull; *however*, Linden is exciting.

3. Linden is exciting. Stonecreek, *in contrast*, is dull.

Look at this example of an often misused transitional expression:

Stonecreek isn't a big town at all. *On the contrary*, it is quite small.

On the contrary is used to describe a surprising fact—something *contrary* to our expectations—about one place. For example:

The people of Stonecreek aren't boring. *On the contrary*, they are quite interesting.

Conjunctions (Subordinators)

1. Stonecreek is small, *whereas* Linden is large.

2. *While* Stonecreek is small, Linden is large.

<u>Conjunctions (Coordinators)</u>

1. Stonecreek is small, *but* Linden is large.

2. Linden is large, *yet* Stonecreek is small.

<u>Prepositions and Prepositional phrases</u>

1. *Unlike* Stonecreek, Linden has many traffic problems.

2. Stonecreek has few traffic problems *in contrast to* Linden.

3. Linden is *different from* Stonecreek in its traffic problems.

Showing Similarities

<u>Transitions</u>

1. Stonecreek has many famous buildings; *likewise*, Linden has much to offer tourists.

2. Linden has a town hall built in 1891. Stonecreek, *similarly*, has a town hall dating from the end of the nineteenth century.

3. Stonecreek's residents are very friendly. *In the same way*, the people of Linden are easy to get to know.

<u>Conjunctions (Coordinators)</u>

1. *Both* Stonecreek *and* Linden have much to offer tourists.

2. *Neither* Linden *nor* Stonecreek has a drug problem.

3. *Not only* Linden *but also* Stonecreek have famous buildings.

<u>Prepositions and Prepositional phrases</u>

1. Stonecreek's town hall is *like* Linden's.

2. Linden is *similar to* Stonecreek in having many tourist attractions.

▶ *Practice 10* **Selecting Linking Words**

Choose the best linking expressions to complete the paragraph. Use the punctuation marks to help you select an appropriate expression.

Water Skiing and Snow Skiing

There are some similarities, but there are more differences between water skiing and snow skiing. First of all, water skiers use two skis to stand on; _____, snow skiers fasten their boots to two long skis. In
A. similarly   B. like   C. however

addition, _____ water skiers, snow skiers bend their knees and
A. alike   B. like   C. in contrast to

use their bodies to turn the skis from one side to the other. As a third similarity,

water skiing is _____ snow skiing in the speed at which it is
A. similarly   B. similar   C. similar to

performed. _____, the two sports also have some
A. Whereas   B. On the other hand   C. In contrast to

obvious differences. _____ water skiing can only take place when
A. While   B. Yet   C. Instead of

it is reasonably warm, snow skiing requires cold weather. Second,

_____ a water skier, a snow skier usually needs two poles
A. on the other hand   B. however   C. unlike

for support and control. Another difference lies in the way performers of the sports

get their speed. Water skiers are pulled behind a speedboat on a flat water surface;

_____, downhill skiers push off from the top of a hill and rely
A. while   B. however   C. differently

on gravity to make them glide down. A snow skier also uses his or her body in a

different way. _____ the water skier, who leans his body
A. Unlike   B. Similar to   C. Both

backward while holding on to a rope, the downhill skier crouches down as far as

possible to minimize wind resistance. Finally, a water skier is evaluated on the basis

of style as well as speed, _____ for a snow skier, style is
A. but   B. different from   C. unlike

unimportant. Only time counts. As a result, a person who is quite good at one

sport may find that the other isn't quite as easy as he or she might have thought.

▶ *Practice 11* Writing Sentences Using Linking Words of Comparison or Contrast

Below are ten characteristics of two pets. *Midnight* is a cat, and *Blaze* is a dog. Choose some of the following characteristics, and on page 162 write six sentences about the two animals. Use expressions of similarity and difference. Make sure to use different linking words in each sentence.

Midnight	**Blaze**
1. ten years old	1. six years old
2. female	2. male
3. responds to her name	3. comes when you call
4. long black fur	4. short brown-and-white fur
5. very active	5. athletic
6. prefers to stay at home	6. loves to sleep on the couch
7. mischievous	7. easygoing
8. loves to play	8. loves to eat
9. has had four babies	9. has never been a father
10. likes strangers	10. enjoys meeting new people

1. _____

_____

2. _____

_____

3. _____

_____

4. _____

_____

5. _____

_____

6. _____

_____

▶ Writing To Communicate

Choose one of these three topics and write a comparison-and-contrast essay. If none of them appeal to you, ask your teacher if you can choose a topic from "Other Essays" on pages 165–166.

1. The Child Is the Father to the Man

In the freewriting exercise on page 152, you compared yourself as a child to the person you are now. Even though you are the same person, this is a lot like comparing two different people. Do you feel that you are very different now than you were as a child?

Which aspects of a person are likely to change as that person grows older? Physical appearance is an obvious point of comparison. You are certainly taller now than you were when you were a child. Below are a few other points you might think about as topics of comparison between the adult you are and the child you were. Add other topics as they relate to you in particular.

- dreams and aspirations

- attitude about life

- physical abilities

- interests

- friends

- relationship with your family

- _____

- _____

- _____

2. My Friend and Me

For this topic, write an essay with a classmate comparing the two of you. You may want to use the areas of appearance, interests, and skills that you used in several exercises in Chapter 12. Follow this process:

1. Start thinking: What do you two have in common?

2. What are your major differences?

3. Think about situations that are or have been examples of the points you just listed.

4. Do your differences outweigh your similarities, or vice versa? Write a thesis statement based on your answer to this question.

5. Can you think of some interesting facts as an introduction to this essay?

6. Write your essay together following an outline. When writing your essay, use the third person ("He is . . . She likes to . . .")

3. Sculptures

Consider these two famous sculptures. What are some of their similarities? Think about the material they are made from, the subject they portray, or the feeling they give you. They are also quite different. What are some of those differences?

Similarities   **Differences**

_____   _____

_____   _____

_____   _____

_____   _____

_____   _____

_____   _____

_____   _____

_____   _____

Look back at Chapter 8: The Introductory Paragraph. Check the type of introduction you want for this essay.

_____ Anecdote   _____ Historical

_____ Interesting fact   _____ General to specific

Write your proposed thesis statement here:

_____

_____

What will your conclusion be?

_____ Summary   _____ Restatement   _____ Final comment

Now, write your essay. Revise and edit it before you share it with another student or hand it in.

Peer Help Worksheet

Check off each step as you complete it.

1 ▶ What did you particularly like about this essay?

2 ▶ Content

Are there additional examples or other changes
that could be made in a revision? . . . . ❑

3 ▶ Organization

a. What kind of introduction is used in this essay?

_____ . . . . ❑

b. Does the essay have _____ mostly differences or _____ mostly
similarities? (Check one.)

c. How many body paragraphs are there? _____ . . . . ❑

d. What kind of organization is used? (Check one.)

Basic block . . . . ❑
Block comparison . . . . ❑
Point-by-point . . . . ❑
Unclear . . . . ❑

e. What kind of conclusion is used? (Check all that apply.)

Restatement . . . . ❑
Summary of main points . . . . ❑
Final comments . . . . ❑
Other . . . . ❑

4 ▶ Editing

Is the grammar and punctuation of each of the transitions
correct? Underline anything you think is incorrect. . . . . ❑

Other Essays

Here are some other topics that lend themselves to a comparison-and-contrast
organizational pattern. Choose one and write an essay about it.

1. Your parents probably led quite different lives in their youth than you do
now. Write an essay comparing your lifestyle with your mother's or father's.
For example:

• In what kind of house did your parent live compared to the one you
live in today?

- Did your parent go to school or work at your age?

- What was your parent's attitude toward freedom of choice compared to yours?

- What were your parent's values compared to yours?

2. Think about a book you have read or a movie you have seen that was based on a book you have read. Pick two books or select a book and its movie version and compare and/or contrast them. For example:

- How were the main characters similar or different?

- What did the plots (the stories) of the two books or book and movie have in common? How were they different?

- How was the setting similar or different?

3. Compare your hometown with where you live now. For example:

- Are the houses and apartments similar or different?

- Can you compare the roads and traffic patterns?

- How do the parks and open areas compare with those of your hometown? Are the trees and plants similar or different? Do people use these areas in the same way?

APPENDIX 1 Writing Under Time Pressure

Taking Essay Exams

Many of the tests you will take at your college or university will include questions that require an essay answer. These "essay answers" aren't necessarily organized like the essays you learned about in this book. An essay answer can be as short as a five-sentence paragraph or as long as several pages. The major difference between this type of writing and the paragraph and essay writing that we've discussed in this book is, of course, time. You are expected to write these essay answers during class in a limited amount of time. With the pressure on, it is natural that you will not have as much control over grammar and punctuation as you do when you have a lot of time to write. However, there are simple guidelines that you can follow that will help you maintain your overall organization and, in this way, make your essay answer clear and understandable. Most professors can overlook a few spelling and minor punctuation mistakes; after all, even native speakers make these kinds of errors sometimes. However, if your answer is hard to follow and your professor has serious trouble understanding what you are trying to say, your grade will most likely be affected.

First, we should say something about test taking in general. Before you begin to write, you should look over the entire test and plan your time. Often, college and university tests have two types of questions: objective and subjective. The objective questions have answers that are either right or wrong and include question types such as true/false, multiple choice, and matching. The subjective questions require essay-type responses and are evaluated by your professor. These question types include definition, short answer, and essay. Another step you should take before actually writing is to note the point value given to each section of the test. This information will also help you plan your test-taking time.

In general, it is a good idea to go through the objective questions rather quickly and leave the bulk of your time for the subjective questions. Some people prefer to tackle the most difficult essay questions first to get them over with; others prefer to do the easier questions first in order to get "on a roll." Do whatever is best for you. Also, try to leave some time at the end to reread your essay responses. Students often catch a lot of mistakes at this point because they can look at their writing more objectively.

In short, the most important point to remember is that it is usually *not* a good idea to take a test from beginning to end, starting when the professor says "go" and stopping when the professor says "time's up." Remember that everyone thinks differently and has a different path to success. Be sure to choose the path that works best for you.

Some Guidelines for Essay-type Questions

- First of all, be aware that some essay questions are not asked in question form. Often, they start with an imperative verb that tells you to do something. Some common verbs used in essay-type questions and their meanings are listed here:

  1. Analyze
     Separate a topic into smaller parts and explain each part

  2. Compare or Contrast
     Tell what is alike or different about two or more topics

  3. Define
     Tell what a word or idea means

  4. Discuss
     Give information about a topic

  5. Explain or Describe
     Tell how something works or what something is like

  6. Summarize
     Tell the most important parts of a topic

  7. Synthesize
     Put information together so that it is easy to understand

- Answer the question in the first one or two sentences of your response. A professor wants to know from the beginning that you are on the right track. Do *not* spend time writing an introductory paragraph. Remember that your time is limited. In addition, you don't have to get the reader's attention. Your professor is a captive audience.

- You also don't need to spend a lot of time writing a concluding paragraph. Just make sure you cover all your points in the main body of the essay.

- Organize your response in a coherent, cohesive fashion. Don't start writing without a plan in mind. Keep your organization simple. Use a basic type of organization, such as process, classification, cause and effect, or comparison and contrast.

- Keep your response on target. In other words, don't just write down everything you know about the topic. Often, this is a signal to professors that you don't really understand the question and are hoping that the answer is somewhere in your response.

- Keep in mind that an important part of higher education in the United States is training students to compile and synthesize information. If you want to get an "A," don't just repeat what the professor has said in class or what you have read in a textbook. Instead, synthesize the two and add some observations of your own.

Writing Essays for Standardized Tests

Many of the standardized tests, such as the TOEFL® test, that are required for admission to a university or college include a short, essay-type response to a question. Often, you will have thirty minutes to answer this type of question. It may ask you about a social, political, or environmental issue, or it may ask you to write about an experience that you have had. The main difference between this type of essay and those you will write for tests once you get into school is that a standardized test question almost always asks you to state and explain your opinion about something.

The main purpose of a writing sample on a standardized test is to show the *test giver* whether or not the *test taker* can communicate his or her opinions in an organized, well-written way. Therefore, many of the guidelines that were discussed previously are also important to remember when taking this type of test.

Some Guidelines for Writing Essays on Standardized Tests

- Often, the essay topic will be given to you, so you should be prepared to write about almost anything! TOEFL® publishes a list of possible topics in its registration brochure, which many people review ahead of time. Since there are usually more than 100 topics listed, you won't be able to think about all of them. However, reviewing the list will help you begin to think about potential topics.

- Before you begin writing, think about what you are going to say. Some tests allow you to use scrap paper to jot down notes. Be absolutely sure that you are responding to what the test question is asking. As you are writing, remember to stick to the point. Two of the most important criteria for evaluating this type of test are whether the writing is unified and whether it responds to the question.

- Also before writing, think about an overall plan of organization. You can choose to write in a paragraph pattern (a topic sentence, supporting sentences, and a concluding sentence) or an essay pattern (an introductory paragraph with thesis statement, body paragraphs, and a concluding paragraph). The choice you make will probably depend on how much time you have, what the topic is, and how comfortable you feel writing in English. The key here, though, is to write a well-organized composition that has a short beginning, a well-supported middle, and (if time allows) a short end.

- Using your time effectively on this type of test is very important. Always bring a watch or clock with you to a standardized test, and check the time periodically. For a thirty-minute test, a good way to organize your time is:

    five minutes: thinking and planning (organizing)

    twenty minutes: writing

    five minutes: rereading and checking for mistakes

- You may not think it is important to take the time to reread what you have written, but it can be of great benefit. Even if you can spend only two or three minutes rereading, you may catch some grammar or spelling errors that can be easily corrected. Often, these are simple errors that even native speakers make when writing under time pressure but that can detract from your message and your grade.

APPENDIX 2 The University Application Essay

Colleges and universities in the United States want to attract the kinds of students who will be successful in their studies. Often, however, they receive applications from many more prospective students than they can accept. As a result, schools need to be very selective when they choose among their applicants. One of the most important factors in their selection is the application essay. There are many different types of college application essay questions, or "prompts." In general, the prompts tend to be of the following four types:

- A self-statement
- An important experience or achievement in your life
- An analysis of a social, political, or moral issue
- A discussion of your career goals

Organizing Your Essay

A Self-Statement

This essay type asks you to tell something about yourself. You might be asked to respond to prompts such as *Tell us something about yourself,* or *Write a one-page essay that gives us a sense of what is important in your life,* or *In 500 words, describe yourself as a good friend would describe you.* Because the essay topic is so general, it is critical that you be selective in your choice of what to include. In this book, you have practiced writing clear thesis statements, writing coherently and cohesively, and selecting relevant and illustrative content to support your assertions. Don't try to write a complete autobiography; this is an exercise in choosing two or three important things about yourself and demonstrating how they have shaped you. Keep in mind that schools are looking for students who are mature, creative, and show leadership potential. This is your chance to sell yourself to the admissions committee!

An Important Experience or Achievement in Your Life

Schools that choose this essay prompt want to know *why* an experience was important and how what you learned from the experience will help you to be successful at that school. For example, you might be asked to respond to prompts such as *Describe an obstacle you have overcome and what you have learned from this experience,* or *What is your most significant scholastic or personal achievement?,* or *Describe a person who has had a special influence on your life.*

The experience or achievement doesn't have to be something as obvious as winning the Student-of-the-Year Award. In fact, your good grades and your teachers' recommendations already show that you are a good student. You should choose something that goes beyond getting good grades, such as overcoming a personal obstacle or getting a job you worked hard for. Notice that the prompt says *an* important experience, not several experiences, so be sure to select just one. Remember to draw a conclusion showing how the experience will make you a valuable addition to that school.

An Analysis of a Social, Political, or Moral Issue

This essay type describes an issue and asks you to analyze it. Sometimes the essay prompt asks you to select a topic that you feel is important, for example, *Do you think the relationship between adults and teenagers has changed in the last fifty years? If yes, how has this relationship influenced your life choices?*, or *In your opinion, what is the most serious issue humanity will face in this century?*, or *Describe an issue of social or political importance and take a stand.*

Since the purpose of the essay is to give the school a sense of your personality as well as of your writing style, be sure not to choose a topic that is too general. It is much better to discuss a topic that you have had personal experience with, such as reducing or increasing the driver's license age, peer pressure, or how an environmental issue has affected your life. Write about what you know; that's what most people do best.

A Discussion of Your Career Goals

No one expects high school students to have their career from college to retirement clearly mapped out. In fact, a school might not be very interested in a person who shows such single-mindedness. It is also not a good idea to say "I want to be a doctor because my parents are forcing me to study medicine" or "I want to be a doctor because all I want to do is to make lots of money." The trick in this essay is to first select a category of jobs, such as designing, health service, computer programming, business management, education, or another general area. Then, write about why you feel drawn to that field and how you have chosen the programs at that particular school to meet your interests. Typical prompts for this type of essay include *What will your intended major be and why?*, or *What do you see yourself doing ten years from now?*, or *How will your studies at XYZ university have an impact on your future career plans?*

APPENDIX 3 Computer Formatting

Submitting handwritten assignments is no longer an option in universities and colleges in the United States. It is expected that all papers will be done on a computer or typewriter. In fact, some professors prefer that students submit their assignments via e-mail, thus eliminating the hard copy altogether. Below is a list of formatting guidelines. Following the list is a sample paper.

1. The margins should be set at an inch on all sides (top, bottom, right, and left).

2. The text is generally justified on the left, which means that each line comes out even at the left margin. You may also choose "block" justification, which means that the text will be even on both the left and right margins.

3. Use a common font, such as Times New Roman, Arial, or Courier. Always use a point size between 12 and 14 points.

4. The name, date, and course title should be placed in the upper right-hand corner. You may also include the professor's name below the course title. If you have multiple pages, put your last name and the page number (starting with 2) in the upper right-hand corner.

5. The title should be centered and spaced one line below the course title (or the professor's name) and one line from the beginning of the paper. Use the word-processing program's centering icon to center the title.

6. Your paper should be double-spaced. It is not necessary to have extra space between paragraphs.

7. The first line of each paragraph should be indented five spaces or .5 inches.

8. The first letter of each sentence is capitalized. Leave one space between each word. There are no spaces between the last word and the period.

9. There are no spaces between a word and a comma or between a word and a semicolon. Leave one space after commas and semicolons.

10. Leave one or two spaces between sentences.

11. In word-processing programs, sentences automatically continue onto the next line when there is not enough space for a word. Do not press "Enter" at the end of a line unless, for example, you want to start a new paragraph.

12. Many word-processing programs automatically indicate when a word is misspelled. Some programs also check grammar. Although these tools are very helpful, be careful. Many will not highlight correctly spelled words that are incorrectly used. For example, if you type *to* when you meant to use *too*, your program may not indicate that it is wrong because *to* is a correctly spelled word. Therefore, no matter how much you trust your computer program, be sure to proofread your work.

Here is an example of a well-formatted academic paper.

Name

Date

Course

Small Things

Three of my experiences in the United States stand out in my memory as typically American. First of all, I remember coming down to breakfast at my host family's house on my first day there. My host mother had already left for work, her two children were eating some cereal, and their father was talking on the phone. He smiled at me and pointed to the refrigerator. I didn't understand, so I just smiled back. I went to school hungry that day. The second experience was trying to take a shower. I had no idea what the different knobs were for and struggled for about half an hour. Finally, I gave up and took a cold bath. The third incident occurred later that week when I went to the supermarket to get some groceries. In my country, we always put our purchases in bags ourselves. When someone else started putting my groceries into a bag, I thought she was stealing my food so I tried to hold on to it. When I finally realized what was going on, I was so embarrassed that I didn't think I could ever go into that store again. These three experiences showed me how cultural differences are often most obvious in minor, everyday events.

APPENDIX 4 Punctuation

Reviewing the Rules

Academic writing follows certain generally accepted rules of punctuating with periods, commas, and semicolons. Below is a list of abbreviations that will be used to discuss the rules of punctuation.

ic = independent clause, or sentence (a group of words that contains a subject and a verb and that can stand alone)

cc = coordinating conjunction (*for, and, nor, but, or, yet, so*)

t = transition (e.g., *however, moreover, therefore*)

ac = adverbial clause (begins with a subordinating conjunction)

z = anything which is the same grammatical structure

Using Commas

- With Coordinating Conjunctions

  When a coordinating conjunction connects two independent clauses, use a comma before the conjunction.

  > Ic, cc ic.

  Example: Jonas is very shy, <u>so</u> he never goes to parties.

- With Transitions

  Use a comma around a transition no matter where it appears in a sentence (at the beginning, in the middle, or at the end).

  > T, ic.
  >
  > Ic [first part], t, ic [second part].
  >
  > Ic, t.

  Examples: Jonas is very shy. <u>However</u>, his brother is an extrovert.
  Jonas is very shy. His brother, <u>however</u>, is an extrovert
  Jonas is very shy. His brother is an extrovert, <u>however</u>.

- With Adverbial Clauses

  Use a comma after an adverbial clause preceding the subject of an independent clause. However, if the adverbial clause comes after the independent clause, don't use a comma.

  > Ac, ic.
  >
  > Ic ac.

  Examples: <u>Because Jonas is very shy</u>, he never goes to parties.
  Jonas never goes to parties <u>because he is very shy</u>.

There is an exception to this rule. When an adverbial clause beginning with the subordinators *whereas* or *while* comes after an independent clause, use a comma.

Examples: Whereas Jonas is very shy, his brother is an extrovert.
Jonas' brother is an extrovert, whereas Jonas is very shy.

- In Lists

Use commas to separate three or more items in a list. Note that the comma before the word *and* is optional.

z, z, and z

OR

z, z and z

Examples: We had meat, potatoes, and corn for dinner.
Tom went to the University of Illinois because he liked the climate, admired its professors, and thought highly of its medical school.
My favorite classes are English, history and biology.

Using Semicolons

Two independent clauses which are closely connected in meaning may be connected with a semicolon. In addition, transitions joining two independent clauses may be preceded by a semicolon and followed by a comma.

Ic; ic.

Ic; t, ic.

Examples: Jonas is very shy; he never goes to parties.
Jonas is very shy; therefore, he never goes to parties.

Punctuation Problems

Both native and non-native speakers of English make three common errors in punctuating sentences: fragments, comma splices, and run-on sentences.

Fragments

A **fragment** is a phrase or a part of a sentence that is incomplete. The minimum sentence in English must contain a subject and a verb with a tense. (Imperatives are special cases.) Four common fragment problems are:

1. a dependent clause

   Example: Because it was hot outside.

2. a phrase without a verb with a tense

   Example: John going to the store.

3. a phrase without a subject

   Example: Went to the store yesterday.

4. a noun phrase without a verb

Example: An air-conditioned car.

These fragment problems can be solved in the following ways:

1. attach the dependent clause to an independent clause
    Correction: John drove to the store because it was hot outside.

OR

Because it was hot outside, John drove to the store.

2. change the verb form to include a tense
    Correction: John was going to the store.

3. add a subject
    Correction: John went to the store yesterday.

4. add a verb and decide if the noun phrase is the subject or object
    Correction: John has an air-conditioned car.

Comma Splices

A **comma splice** occurs when a comma is used by itself between two independent clauses.

Example: I went to my friend's house, he wasn't home.

There are four common ways to correct comma splices:

1. substitute a period for the comma
    Correction: I went to my friend's house. He wasn't home.

2. substitute a semicolon for the comma
    Correction: I went to my friend's house; he wasn't home.

3. add a coordinating conjunction
    Correction: I went to my friend's house, but he wasn't home.

4. change one of the clauses to a dependent clause by starting it with a subordinating conjunction
    Correction: Even though I went to my friend's house, he wasn't home.

Run-on Sentences

A **run-on sentence** occurs when two or more independent clauses (plus possible dependent clauses) follow each other without punctuation. Run-ons must be separated into independent and dependent clauses and punctuated properly.

Example: I didn't have enough milk in the house yesterday so I went to the store to buy some the store was closed so I drove to my friend's house but he wasn't at home I decided not to eat breakfast.

To correct a run-on sentence, add commas and periods.

Correction: I didn't have enough milk in the house yesterday, so I went to the store to buy some. The store was closed, so I drove to my friend's house, but he wasn't at home. I decided not to eat breakfast.

APPENDIX 5 Common Linking Words

	Transitions	Conjunctions		Prepositions
		Subordinate	**Coordinate**	
Chronology	first, second, etc. first of all at first next after that later on at last finally then eventually	after before while when since	and or	after before since prior to
Description	nearby			on top of under to the left to the right in front of behind above next to
Example	for example for instance			such as
Causation		because since as	for	because of due to
Result	therefore for this reason as a result/consequence consequently hence		so	
Unexpected Result	however nevertheless nonetheless	even though although	but yet	in spite of despite

	Transitions	Conjunctions		Prepositions
		Subordinate	Coordinate	
Contrast	however in contrast		but yet	in contrast to instead of different from
Direct Contrast	on the other hand however	whereas while	but yet	unlike
Similarity	likewise similarly in the same way		both . . . and neither . . . nor not only . . . but also	like similar to
Explanation	in other words that is			
Emphasis	indeed in fact			
Addition	in addition furthermore moreover			in addition to
Condition	otherwise in this case	if		
Conclusion	in conclusion to sum up in short all in all			

APPENDIX 6 General Peer Help Worksheet

The Paragraph Checklists and Peer Help Worksheets that appear throughout this book were designed to help you look at your writing with a critical eye. Many of the checklists and worksheets in the book focus on one particular topic, but the worksheet below is more general and can be used to help you evaluate any academic essay.

General Peer Help Worksheet

Check off each step as you complete it.

1 What did you particularly like about this essay?

2 Content:
  a. What is the rhetorical pattern used in this essay? _____ ... ☐
  b. Do the individual paragraphs have unity? Underline sentences you think are irrelevant. .... ☐

3 Organization:
  a. What kind of introductory paragraph does this essay have? (Check one.)
    Personal anecdote .... ☐
    Third-person anecdote .... ☐
    Interesting fact or statistic .... ☐
    Historical introduction .... ☐
    General to specific .... ☐
    Other (specific to rhetorical pattern) .... ☐
  b. Underline the thesis statement. Circle the controlling idea. Put a box around the predictor, if any. .... ☐
  c. Do the body paragraphs have good coherence? .... ☐
  d. What elements of concluding paragraphs does the concluding paragraph in this essay have? (Check all that apply.)
    Summary .... ☐
    Restatement of the thesis statement .... ☐
    Final comment .... ☐

4 Editing
  a. Check for the appropriate use of capital letters, periods, commas, and semicolons. .... ☐
  b. Check for problems with fragments, comma splices, and run-on sentences. .... ☐

APPENDIX 7 Paragraph and Essay Evaluation

There are many things to consider when evaluating academic writing. While different teachers and schools will use their own evaluation tools, most will include categories similar to those outlined in the form below.

SCORING		ASPECTS OF GOOD WRITING	
Exceptional:	25–23	Content/Ideas	
Very good:	22–20	• has excellent support	
Average:	19–17	• is interesting to read	
Needs work:	16–0	• has unity and completeness	
SCORE:		• adheres to assignment parameters	
Exceptional:	25–23	Organization	
Very good:	22–20	**Paragraph**	**Essay**
Average:	19–17	• has topic sentence with clear controlling idea	• has introductory paragraph with clear thesis statement
Needs work:	16–0	• has supporting sentences	• has body paragraphs with good organization
		• has concluding sentence	• has concluding paragraph
SCORE:		• has coherence and cohesion	• has coherence and cohesion
Exceptional:	25–23	Grammar/Structure	
Very good:	22–20	• demonstrates control of basic grammar (e.g., tenses, verb forms, noun forms, preposition, articles)	
Average:	19–17	• shows sophistication of sentence structure with complex and compound sentences	
Needs work:	16–0		
SCORE:			
Exceptional:	15–14	Word Choice/Word Form	
Very good:	13–12	• demonstrates sophisticated choice of vocabulary items	
Average:	11–10	• has correct idiomatic use of vocabulary	
Needs work:	9–0	• has correct word forms	
SCORE:			
Exceptional:	10	Mechanics	
Very good:	9–8	• has good paragraph format	
Average:	7–6	• demonstrates good control over use of capital letters, periods, commas, and semicolons	
Needs work:	5–0	• demonstrates control over spelling	
SCORE:		• doesn't have fragments, comma splices, or run-on sentences	
TOTAL SCORE:		Comments	

APPENDIX 8 Suggested Correction Symbols

Below is a list of common correction symbols used when evaluating an academic paper. Your teacher may use other symbols as well. Be sure to ask about any symbols you do not understand.

cap	Mistake in use of capital letter(s): add or delete
c	Mistake in use of commas: add or delete
p	Mistake in punctuation (semicolon or period): add or delete
ℙ	Mistake in paragraph format
sp	Spelling mistake
ref	Unclear reference of pronoun
ww	Wrong word
wf	Wrong form of word
wo	Wrong word order
t	Mistake in verb tense and/or aspect
voc	Mistake in use of active or passive voice
art	Mistake in article use
prep	Mistake in preposition use
agr	Mistake in agreement of subject and verb
#	Mistake in number (singular/plural)
poss	Mistake in use of possessive form
∧	Omission (word[s] missing)
X	Drawn through a word, this indicates that the word should be omitted.
frag	Sentence fragment
rs	Run-on sentence
cs	Comma splice
inf	Too informal for academic writing
?	Unclear passage or sentence. Ask your teacher.
OK	Teacher mistake. Ignore it.

ANSWER KEY

Note: For exercises where no answers are given, answers will vary.

Chapter 2

▶ **Practice 1,** page 8

1. D   2. N   3. N   4. E   5. D

Chapter 3

▶ **Practice 1,** page 20

1. <u>Alcohol</u> (is harmful to your health.)
2. <u>The Western world</u> (should have a holiday to recognize senior citizens.)
3. <u>The colors of the U.S. flag</u> (have unique symbolic meanings.)
4. <u>A camping vacation</u> (sounds like a punishment to me.)
5. <u>Weeds</u> (can ruin a vegetable garden.)

▶ **Practice 2,** page 20

1. <u>American education</u> (has five stages.)
2. ~~My brother is older than I am.~~
3. <u>Writing a good résumé</u> (takes a lot of hard work.)
4. ~~Jack is Kate's friend.~~
5. <u>Jack</u> (is Kate's best friend.)
6. (You need four ingredients) <u>to make peanut butter.</u>
7. <u>Big business</u> (is threatening the environment.)
8. ~~Big business has an effect on the environment.~~
9. ~~Cats are also called felines.~~
10. There are (many) <u>reasons to visit San Francisco.</u>

▶ **Practice 4,** page 23

TS
Usually three or four weeks before Valentine's day, you begin to see too many reminders of this only-for-lovers holiday almost everywhere.

    SS
    For example, you see red hearts and cupids in every shop and restaurant.

        ss
        Shops want you to buy a gift for your Valentine, and restaurants hope that you will treat yourself and your Valentine to an expensive dinner.

SS

You also seem to see more pictures of people in love and more people on the streets who are obviously in love.

> **ss**
>
> They walk hand-in-hand and gaze into each other's eyes lovingly.

SS

Another example of Valentine's Day reminders is seeing the commercials on TV, which tell you about all the wonderful presents and cards that you can buy for that "special someone."

CS

In short, we are constantly reminded of Valentine's Day for several weeks each year.

▶ *Practice 5,* **page 25** *Suggested responses. Student responses may vary.*

1. In summary, when the decorations are put up too early, it diminishes the meaning of the holiday.

2. In short, my first day in kindergarten was a lot more difficult than entering college.

3. All in all, my first car was gorgeous to me.

▶ *Practice 6,* **page 26**

1. In the United States religious holidays often become non religious.

2. The government of the United States recognizes eight holidays by giving its employees the day off.

3. ~~the parents hiding several hundred Easter eggs~~

4. ~~when we spent a long holiday weekend in the mountains~~

5. Most people look forward to long holiday weekends.

▶ *Practice 7,* **page 27**

1. David is allergic to cats, so he doesn't have one.

2. You can have cereal for breakfast, or you can have eggs for breakfast.

3. Ken loves to celebrate New Year's Eve, but he's too sick to go out this year.

4. The roses in the garden are dying, for they aren't getting enough water.

5. The sun isn't shining brightly, nor is it completely hidden.

6. Katy went to Colorado, and she rafted down the Colorado River.

7. The bird is looking for small branches to build a nest, yet she can't find any.

Chapter 4 ————————————————————————

▶ *Practice 1,* **page 34**

2. D = descriptive. Circle the sentence "The ears had green earrings" and move it to follow the sentence "The head had two bright red ears that stood straight up."

3. N = narrative. Circle the sentence "That evening, we went dancing at the old Starlight Room downtown" and move it to follow the sentence "The owners of the theater had even managed to find out what was playing the day of their wedding, so we watched the same movie they had."

4. E = expository. Circle the sentence "Examples of string instruments are violins, cellos, and basses" and move it to follow the sentence "Their sound is produced by vibrating strings or wires."

▶ *Practice 2,* **page 38**

Traveling to a foreign city can be fun, but **it** requires some planning besides getting a passport. **First,** you should buy a phrase book and learn a few key phrases in **the** foreign language. Using **these** phrases demonstrates a willingness to learn about **the** people who live in the foreign city. **Second,** read about **the** city beforehand and read about the places in **it** you'd like to see. Get a feeling for **it** and for **its** weather so that you can pack appropriate clothes. **Next,** check your camera. Make sure that **it** is in good working order and that you have lots film. **Finally,** get yourself a good pair of walking shoes and break **them** in for about a month before you leave. **In short,** taking a few precautions before you leave can make your trip to a foreign city more enjoyable.

▶ *Practice 3,* **page 40** *Suggested responses. Student responses may vary.*

1. The Pacific Ocean has many forms if life. For example, there are fish, plants, and microscopic plankton.

2. First, I dragged myself out of bed. Then, I took a cold shower to wake myself up.

3. December is a winter month in the Northern Hemisphere. However, it is a summer month in the Southern Hemisphere.

4. The volcano erupted for ten days. As a result, the village at the bottom of it was destroyed.

5. If you want to enjoy a long holiday weekend, you need to leave for your destination early. Furthermore, you need to come back early.

▶ *Practice 4,* **page 41** *Suggested responses. Student responses may vary.*

1. Because Monday is the Fourth of July, we don't have to go to work.

2. Although fireworks are standard for holiday celebrations, I don't like them.

3. While it is foggy and cold near the ocean, it is sunny and hot inland.

4. After Betty baked some Christmas cookies, she took them to her neighbor.

5. There will soon be too many people in the world if people keep having babies.

Chapter 5 ——————————————————————————————

▶ *Practice 1,* **page 45**

1. Irrelevant sentence: "Today, many tourists visit both canals."

2. Irrelevant sentence: "She was a great asset to her husband, Franklin, who was president of the United States from 1932 to 1945."

▶ Practice 2, page 46

1. Irrelevant sentence: "Some millionaires killed themselves because they lost all their money."

2. Irrelevant sentence: "There is also a Fantasyland at Disney World in Florida."
   Irrelevant sentence: "Now, of course, there are many more roller coasters in Disneyland, such as Space Mountain and Thunder Mountain."

3. No irrelevant sentences.

▶ Practice 3, page 48

1. The topic sentence describes two officially declared wars. The writer of the paragraph has omitted mention of World War II. Some sentences describing WWII need to be added.

2. Complete.

3. The paragraph describes how the rider got the first twenty-five miles and then the next twenty-five miles. However, the writer says that by the end of the day, the rider had covered seventy-five miles. We need a sentence or two describing the last leg of the journey.

▶ Practice 4, page 51

Fragment 1: Actually started out in England . . .
Correction: **It** actually started out in England . . .

Fragment 2: By 1830, most urban and rural areas teams that played together . . .
Correction: By 1830, most urban and rural areas **had** teams that played together . . .

Fragment 3: When a group in New York City published a book in 1845.
Correction: When a group in New York City published a book in 1845 **[,]** it gave baseball . . .

Fragment 4: Simply called the New York game.
Correction: Simply called the New York game **[,]** its popularity continued . . .

Fragment 5: By the end of the 1860s.
Correction: By the end of the 1860s **[,]** the name had changed baseball and **it** looked . . .

▶ Practice 5, page 51

1. The paragraph shows good coherence because the sentences are ordered in an expository manner. First, it describes the civil rights movement, then the women's liberation movement, and finally the sexual revolution.

2. There is also good use of cohesive devices. Some examples of sentences with cohesive devises are: <u>This</u> was begun in earnest . . . <u>They</u> demanded to be treated . . . <u>In conclusion</u>, many social movements . . . [Note that these are just three examples. There are other good cohesive devices in the paragraph.]

3. There is one irrelevant sentence: "Both men were killed by assassins." This needs to be removed to restore unity.

4. The paragraph is acceptably complete.

Chapter 6

▶ *Practice 1,* page 59

Topic sentence: Many animals find security in blending in with their environment.

Body: In birds, for example . . . Most fish are darker on top than on the bottom; from above, they look like the land at the bottom of the water, and from below, they look like the water's surface.

Concluding sentence: The safety that these animals' protective coloring provides has helped them survive over the ages.

▶ *Practice 2,* page 59

Introductory paragraph: Animals in the wild have many natural enemies. . . Many animals find security in blending in with their environment.

Supporting paragraph: <u>In birds, for example, although it is quite common for the adult males to be brightly colored and very noticeable, adult females and young chicks are light brown or sand colored to blend into their background and escape the sharp eyes of a predator.</u> This coloring . . . is much less colorful than the male. <u>Adopting camouflage colors helps the female birds survive and raise another generation of birds.</u>

Supporting paragraph: <u>Many mammals have also adopted the colors of their surroundings.</u> A zebra . . . on hunting and feeding her young. <u>All these mammals have, over many years, developed protective coloring to assist them in the struggle to survive.</u>

Supporting paragraph: <u>Most fish are darker on top than on the bottom; from above, they look like the land at the bottom of the water, and from below, they look like the water's surface.</u> Many ocean fish . . . looks like pebbles. <u>Because they look just like their surroundings, these fish survive and avoid becoming someone else's lunch.</u>

Concluding paragraph: Looking like their environment is helpful to these animals for the survival of the species. . . The safety these animals find in their protective coloring has helped them survive over the ages.

▶ *Practice 3,* page 61

Body paragraph 1: Birds

  Major support 1: cardinal

    Minor support: male – bright; female – dull

  Major support 2: peacock

    Minor support: male – bright green and gold, peacock blue; female – peahen – less colorful

Body paragraph 2: Mammals

  Major support 1: zebra

    Minor support: none

  Major support 2: lion

    Minor support: lioness and her young

Body paragraph 3: Fish

Major support 1: ocean fish

Minor support: mackerel

Major support 2: flatfish

Minor support: none

▶ Practice 4, page 63

1. Baby whales stay with their mothers for one to two years[;] after that[,] they usually go out on their own.

2. Loggers in the Northwest cut down the forests[;] consequently[,] they destroy some animals' natural habitats.

3. First[,] we'll feed the dogs[;] later on[,] we'll feed ourselves.

4. The city government is trying many ways to decrease the number of wild cats in the park[;] for instance[,] animal control officers are catching the cats and neutering them.

5. Furthermore[,] the police can suspend your dog's license.

6. Frank seems to hate people[;] on the other hand[,] he is very loving with his cats.

7. Some birds live permanently in the Arctic[;] however[,] most migrate.

8. For example[,] I never leave home without my dogs.

Chapter 7

▶ Practice 1, page 69

1. Topic: Modern methods of building houses
   Controlling idea: have greatly increased their ability to withstand earthquakes
   Predictor: No predictor

2. Topic: Washington, D.C.
   Controlling idea: a fascinating place to visit
   Predictor: beauty, history, and location

3. Topic: there is life on other planets
   Controlling idea: considerable evidence to show
   Predictor: No predictor

4. Topic: houses in my country
   Controlling idea: three characteristics show that it gets very cold there in winter
   Predictor: the thick walls, the two-door entries, and the steep roofs

▶ Practice 2, page 70

1. air; water; soil

2. appearance; effective transportation; open spaces

3. paths; lakes; small forests

▶ **Practice 3,** page 71 *Suggested thesis statements in parentheses.*

1. ✓

2. rule 3 (A Mistubishi is the best Japanese car for several reasons.)

3. rule 4 (Seat belts are necessary to ensure personal safety.)

4. rule 1 (Seat belts are necessary.)

5. ✓

6. rule 5 (Professors work hard for their students.)

7. rule 3 (There are more advantages than disadvantages to working while you are an undergraduate.)

8. ✓

9. rule 2 (An analysis of the university's work study programs shows its clear failure.)

10. rule 4 (Working on campus is ideal for the foreign student.)

▶ **Practice 5,** page 73 *Suggested responses. Student responses may vary.*

Planting roses is easy if you follow these steps. First you need to measure the diameter of the roots[.] [N]ext you must dig a hole twice as big as that diameter. This hole should be so deep that the roots have plenty of room to grow. Mix some rose fertilizer with the soil at the bottom of the hole[;] this is to help the rose to flower later. The next step is to form a little hill in the middle of the hole[.] [Y]ou are going to spread out the roots over the top of this hill. Hold the rose firmly with one hand and spread out the roots with your other hand. Be careful not to break the roots [**since**] they are quite delicate. While you are holding the plant with one hand, pat the soil down gently around the roots. Continue putting soil over the roots until the area around the plant is filled up to a level a little lower than the soil level around it. Finally, water your plant thoroughly. With enough water and some sunshine, you should see your rose plant begin to grow leaves in a few weeks.

▶ **Practice 6,** page 74

Cities can grow in an organic way or in a planned way[.] [O]rganic cities are usually older cities[.] [T]hey are called organic because they have spread in different directions with no precise plan except to accommodate the growing population[.] [O]n the other hand[,] the modern planned cities are sometimes designed before they are even really established[.] [I]n a such a plan[,] careful attention is paid to the amount of residential and commercial spaces[.] [I]n short[,] there are two types of city growth.

Chapter 8

▶ **Practice 1,** page 80

1. a. No; b. N/A; c. It's too general.

2. a. No; b. N/A; c. It previews the content of the body paragraphs of the essay.

3. a. Yes; b. Anecdote; c. N/A

4. a. No; b. N/A; c. It's too short.

► *Practice 4,* **page 83** *Note: The comma preceding the last item in a list is optional.*

2. I'm not sure if my boss went to Bali[,] Fiji[,] or Tahiti on vacation. [nouns]

3. Across the street[,] behind the house[,] and under the picnic table, you'll find the last Easter egg. [prepositional phrases]

4. The team played hard[,] made lots of points[,] but lost the game. [verb phrases]

5. Jill Jackson[,] Louis Dana[,] and I ate three pizzas last night. [nouns]

   OR: Jill[,] Jackson[,] Louis[,] Dana[,] and I ate three pizzas last night. [nouns]

6. Jen bought a big[,] floppy[,] blue hat on 18th Street. [adjectives]

Chapter 9

► *Practice 1,* **page 89**

Paragraph 2 is best. Paragraph 1 only paraphrases two of the three major supports. Paragraph 3 adds the topic of weather, which isn't mentioned in the essay.

► *Practice 2,* **page 90** *Note: The comma preceding the last item in a list is optional.*

Correct	Human beings are considered warm-blooded, but snakes and other reptiles are often called cold-blooded.
Incorrect	This is actually not correct ✗because some reptiles maintain their bodies at a higher temperature than
Incorrect	most mammals. However[,] we use the term *cold-blooded* to refer to the fact that most reptiles rely solely on external sources of heat. Reptiles regulate their body temperatures by taking advantage of different sources
Correct/Incorrect	of outside warmth, such as direct sunlight[,] warm stones and the heated earth. Because they use such heat
Correct	sources to varying degrees, individual species of reptiles are able to regulate their body temperature. This body temperature may be above the temperature
Incorrect/Correct	of the surrounding air[,] but when the animal is inactive, the body temperature is approximately the same as that of the environment.

Chapter 10

► *Practice 2,* **page 98**

Thesis statement: <u>Greenpeace has had steady, if small, success in decreasing whale hunting, saving old forests, and cutting down on toxic pollution of our air and water.</u>

Greenpeace works hard to protect the quality of our oceans and their populations of fish, mammals, and vegetation: <u>Not a topic sentence</u>

This very personal type of protest has been successful for Greenpeace elsewhere as well: <u>Bridge</u>

Ancient forests, according to Greenpeace, are forest areas that are relatively undisturbed by human activity: <u>Not a topic sentence</u>

Although this was only a small step in the process of protecting the forests we have left, it was still a significant event: <u>A concluding sentence</u>

However, the major threat to vegetation, animals, and people is now neither hunting nor cutting: <u>Bridge</u>

It is the extremely toxic chemicals that our industrial society releases into both air and water.: <u>Topic sentence</u>

With the help of Greenpeace, the citizens of Convent won their battle in September of 1998, when Shintech withdrew its plans to build the factories: <u>Not a concluding sentence</u>

▶ *Practice 3,* **page 100** *Note: The comma preceding the last item in a list is optional.*

There are three main kinds of animals that people keep in cages or glass tanks so they can watch them: birds[,] reptiles and rodents. Because they are colorful and graceful to look at[,] [b]irds are very popular. In my country, some people have only one big bird in a cage[,] but others have several small ones fluttering and chirping around in a single cage. I would never consider having a reptile, such as a snake, in my house[;] however[,] a friend of mine has a boa constrictor in a cage[ ] and swears that it is a lovely pet[ ] since it doesn't bark[,] doesn't eat much and never needs to be taken out for a walk. Finally, rodents are another kind of animal that can be kept in a cage. Rodents are small animals like guinea pigs[,] gerbils and hamsters[.] [T]hey are especially popular with children. If they are treated properly[,] they can live quite a long time. In short[,] these animals have a fascination for people who mostly like to watch their pets.

Chapter 11 —————————————————————————

▶ *Practice 3,* **page 108**

2. Use of personal pronoun *it.*

3. Use of personal pronoun *me.*

4. Use of personal pronoun *us.*

5. Use of demonstrative pronoun *this.*

6. Use of linking word *therefore.*

7. Use of personal pronoun *I.*

▶ *Practice 4,* **page 109**

Sentence 1: First, break 3 eggs in a bowl.

Sentence 2: Next, mix them using a wire whisk.

Sentences 3 + 4: After you pour in 1 tablespoon of water for each egg, add a pinch of salt.

Sentence 5:   At this point, heat a frying pan.

Sentences 6 + 7:   After you melt 1 tablespoon of butter in the pan, pour in the egg mixture.

Sentences 8 + 9:   Stir the eggs by scraping the pan with a spatula until the eggs are golden yellow.

Sentence 10:   Finally, don't overcook the eggs. Cooking them too long makes them rubbery.

▶ *Practice 5,* **page 110**

When my best friend died in a horrible car accident[,] I thought my heart would be broken forever. It felt like there had been an earthquake and that all my happiness had been crushed beneath a mountain of stones. The way back to life and love was long[,] but I took small steps of improvement along the way. First[,] my mother taught me to appreciate the little things of everyday life, such as the taste of icy cold milk or the smell of my dog's newly washed fur. After a few months[,] I was able to smile at my little sister when she tried so hard to please me. Every week, my grandfather drove me to the cemetery where my friend's grave was[,] and I finally realized how kind he was to me. Much later, I actually went to eat pizza with my classmates and even enjoyed myself. That was when I began to understand that my friend wouldn't have wanted me to fall apart in my unhappiness; he would have wanted me to continue in life. Therefore[,] when I met someone I really liked[,] I agreed to go out with him. It took a whole year, but I have learned to love again.

Chapter 12

▶ *Practice 1,* **page 114**   *Suggested responses. Student responses may vary.*

Subject	Classification Principle	Number of Categories	Category Names
Buildings	material	four	wood, brick, concrete, steel
Paintings	style	three	realistic, impressionistic, abstract
Pets	type of skin	three	fur, feathers, scales

▶ *Practice 2,* **page 115**   *Suggested responses. Student responses may vary.*

Group	Classifying Principle	Number of Categories	Category Names
People	gender	two	male, female
People	height	three	tall, average, short

▶ *Practice 3,* **page 115**

1. c   **2.** b   **3.** a   **4.** b

▶ **Practice 4,** page 116   *Suggested responses. Student responses may vary.*

1. Categories: two, three, four, more than four
   Thesis statement: Vehicles can be easily classified by the number of wheels that they have.

2. Categories: police department, neighborhood watches, private security
   Thesis statement: There are three main providers of protection for people's homes and offices: the police department, neighboorhood watches, and private security.

3. Categories: high school grades, SAT scores, letters of recommendation, extracurricular activities,
   Thesis statement: In order to get into college, you must have four pieces of documentation: your high school grades, your SAT score, one or more letters of recommendation, a history of extracurricular activities.

▶ **Practice 8,** page 120

1. family members   3. three
2. personality types   4. athletic, studious, materialistic

▶ **Practice 9,** page 121

1. relationships between service providers and service consumers
2. the amount of authority of the provider
3. three
4. customer and salesperson, student and teacher, patient and doctor

▶ **Practice 12,** page 125   *Suggested responses. Student responses may vary.*

1. It was miserable weather; as a result, we canceled the picnic.
2. Solar energy is very useful. For instance, it can heat water.
3. I was sick. Consequently, I went to the doctor.
4. Many former U.S. presidents, such as Bill Clinton, continue to lead very active lives.
5. Julie had too much work to do last night. For this reason, she didn't go to the party.

Chapter 13

▶ *Practice 1,* **page 131** *Suggested responses. Student responses may vary.*

Topic	Causes	Effects
Allowing a child to adopt a pet	immediate The child begs for a pet.	expected The child has fun playing with the pet.
	deep The parents are worried that the child has too few friends.	unexpected The child doesn't care about the pet after a few months.
Limiting the number of hours per week that a child can watch TV	immediate The parents think TV watching makes children violent.	expected The child finds other activities.
	deep The parents want the child to spend more time on homework.	unexpected The child searches the Internet for violent games instead.
Talking to teenagers about smoking, drinking alcohol, and using drugs	immediate The parents know that the children's friends are beginning to experiment with drugs.	expected The children follow their parents' example.
	deep The parents don't want the children to make the same mistakes they made.	unexpected The children think their parents are hypocrites.

▶ *Practice 3,* **page 135**

1. "The rules in our house were strict and had both short-term and long-term effects."

2. Block style 3

3. The only cause mentioned is in the introductory paragraph: having ten children.

4. Three effects are discussed: learning to be neat, working hard in school, and close family relationships. Both short-term and long-term effects are mentioned.

▶ *Practice 4,* **page 136**

1. "We can take comfort, however, in the fact that there are many reasons that teenagers rebel against their parents and in the fact that there are also positive effects."

2. Block style 1

3. Three causes: physiological/physical change, psychological change, and peer pressure.

4. Three effects: becoming socialized, forming nonfamily relationships, and becoming confident. The effects discussed are long-term.

▶ *Practice 6,* **page 139**

1. Promoting a sense of teamwork is important; **consequently**, playing sports after school is good for children.
   Promoting a sense of teamwork is important, **so** playing sports after school is good for children.
   Playing sports after school is good for children **due to** the fact that it promotes a sense of teamwork.

2. Teenagers don't want to be punished; **as a result**, they sometimes lie to their parents.
Teenagers sometimes lie to their parents **as** they don't want to be punished.
Because of not wanting to be punished, teenagers sometimes lie to their parents.

3. **Since** the decision to have a baby is very important, it should be given a lot of thought.
Due to its importance, the decision to have a baby should be given a lot of thought.
The decision to have a baby is very important, **so** it should be given a lot of thought.

Chapter 14

▶ *Practice 3,* page 151

Block comparison

▶ *Practice 6,* page 154

1. Towns

2. Location, size, natural beauty, economies, people

3. Point-by-point comparison

4. Three differences; thirteen similarities

▶ *Practice 7,* page 156

1. People

2. Body paragraph 1: Lisa
Body paragraph 2: Ellen

3. Block comparison

4. Personality; family

▶ *Practice 8,* page 157

1. Jobs

2. Body paragraph 1: Similarities among jobs
Body paragraph 2: Differences among jobs

3. Basic block

4. Similarities: part-time work; unskilled work
Differences: amount of mental vs. physical work; amount of independence;
involvement with people or objects

▶ *Practice 9,* page 158

Model Essay 1: Summary, restatement, and final comment
Model Essay 2: Restatement, final comment
Model Essay 3: Summary, restatement, and final comment

▶ *Practice 10,* page 160

A, B, C, B, A, C, B, A, A